The
Story and Tales
of the
BUCHAN LINE

Compiled by

Alan H. Sangster

Oxford Publishing Co.

ISBN 86093 179 X

ACKNOWLEDGEMENT

Thanks is given to the Publishing Committee of the Great North of Scotland
Railway Association for their help and permission to reprint Association
material in this book.

DEDICATION
To my wife Elizabeth and son Donald

Typesetting by:
Aquarius Typesetting Services, New Milton, Hants.

Printed in Great Britain by:
S & S Press, Abingdon, Oxon.

Published by:
Oxford Publishing Co.,
Link House,
West Street,
POOLE, Dorset.

FOREWORD

The railway system in the part of Aberdeenshire known as Buchan is now but a memory with remaining scars of overgrown and derelict track beds and stations. The lines were a small network of branches serving the rural coastal hinterland of the county and served the local industries of agriculture and fishing. In their heyday they were exceptionally busy by rural railway standards and, even to the last, played an important part in the transport of oil-related pipelines to this area of 'black gold'. The final remaining freight service from Aberdeen to Fraserburgh was withdrawn after much local opposition and press publicity in October 1979. The remaining solum of the track bed is the subject of much politics and debate between the Grampian Regional Council and British Rail. The authorities in the region feel strongly that it should be retained with a view to reopening with the impending further large scale growth of the offshore oilfields and plans for refining and gas plants in the Peterhead area.

There is no doubt that British Rail's critical financial plight played a large part in the, perhaps, unnecessary and premature closure of the lines when the area, which has already grown considerably in economic terms in the last 20 years, is set for further large scale industrial expansion in the oil-related field.

This book is not an academic history of the Buchan lines, but a collection, or pot-pourri, of articles covering various aspects of the railway including historical as well as operational matters and plain 'couthy' tales of journeys on the railway which paint a picture of the general atmosphere of the railway in bygone days.

The railway had no special scenic merits to place it in the same class as better known lines, such as the West Highland or Kyle of Lochalsh Railway, but it had its own local rural charm and character which gained it much affection by its users and people in the Aberdeen area.

Throughout this book, reference has been made, on many occasions to the 'Great North'. This is the title by which the Great North of Scotland Railway has become known locally. This book is not written by one author, but by several, all being members of the Great North of Scotland Railway Association. All the articles have been published in the association's *Review* between 1964 and 1979. It is felt that they will prove of interest to a much wider and general readership and will illustrate that collating railway history is much more than purely documenting opening and closing dates and detailing strings of facts and figures.

None of the contributors are professional writers. All are enthusiasts who have done much research and hard work in ensuring the railways they loved are documented and related for posterity.

Alan H. Sangster
Port Erroll Railway
Cruden Bay
Aberdeenshire
1980

MAP of the RAILWAYS of BUCHAN

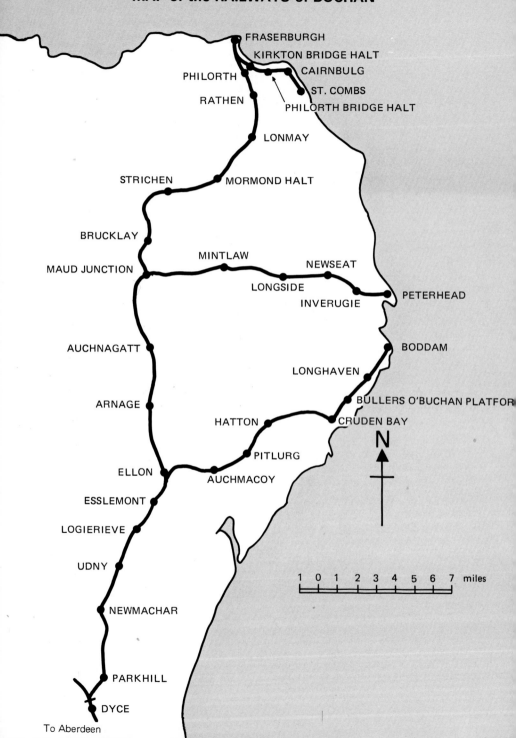

CONTENTS

The 4.02 p.m. Peterhead and Fraserburgh train leaves Aberdeen, on 3rd July 1954, behind Thompson 'B1', No. 61351.

E. C. Haywood

Mr A. Sangster, the author, clerk at Dyce Junction Station in November 1963, stands on the platform. In the background, the 10.05 a.m. from Fraserburgh has just arrived hauled by an NBL Type 2 diesel-electric locomotive.

A. Sangster Collection

BUCHAN LINES
by
Long John

In the bleak Buchan landscape lie the remains of one of the Great North's least successful ventures. Almost the last branch to be built and the first to be closed, the Cruden Bay line, would not be called a great financial success.

It was in 1891 that Mr Woodman Smith, commissioner to the Earl of Erroll, put forward the first scheme for a line to serve the Cruden Bay district. Under this scheme a line was projected which, after leaving the present Buchan line near Udny and crossing the Ythan at Newburgh, would have continued along the coast to Port Errol, or further. However, this scheme was found to be open to some serious objections. In the first place, the cost of the line, about twenty-six miles in all with a large viaduct across the mouth of the Ythan, would have been out of all proportion to the anticipated traffic and in the second place, the situation of the line left a large area of country to the west, between it and the Buchan line, unserved.

The final proposal for the line as it was built appeared in 1892 and met with general approval. With fifteen and a half miles of line required, involving some fairly heavy engineering works and cuttings, the original conservative estimate of £80,000 was passed and the branch was finally opened in August 1897. There were six stations including the halt at Bullers o' Buchan and additionally two sidings were provided to serve the Cruden Brick Company and the Longhaven Quarry.

It could be seen that the sources of traffic for the new line lay in agricultural and fishing produce, the varied material required for the pursuit of these industries, the produce of the quarries and of course passengers.

However, the new line was expected to have a very important effect in quite a new direction. It may be doubted if the Buchan coast had ever been looked on as a fashionable place of retreat, but heartened by their success with the Palace Hotel, the 'Great North' decided to develop Cruden Bay as a luxurious holiday and rest centre.

The large and magnificently appointed hotel was built a short distance from the beach, the ground in front sloping to the sea. A short electric tramway about half a mile long was built from the railway station to take the visitors right to the front door of the hotel and a short branch for laundry and goods going round to the back of the hotel. Tennis courts, croquet lawns and bowling greens were laid out between the front of the building, facing southwards, and the sands, which stretched for miles along the coast, offering to the less active residents the best possible pleasure ground. A special feature of the amenities was the new golf-course which the professionals of the day put on a par with any course north of the Tweed.

The hotel itself was built in the red granite of the district and consisted of a main block with a one hundred foot central tower and projecting wings. A resident of the hotel would find a pleasant lounge at the front entrance which led into a large oak floored hall used at nights for dancing. There was a large coffee room and breakfast room on the west side of the entrance hall and on the east were the reading, writing, drawing and billiard rooms. Special quarters were built for the golfers and bathrooms, heating and drying rooms and lockers gave every convenience and comfort. In the rest of the hotel there were nearly one hundred bedrooms and private suites and, with numerous bathrooms, electric lighting and hydraulic lifts, it was surely the epitome of grace and elegance set amongst salubrious surroundings.

It certainly must have been disheartening to the directors to realize that their grand hotel was a financial failure. In an advertising brochure produced during the early years of this century, the Great North described the hotel in glowing terms and, further to attract visitors, ascribed to the Buchan area a most appealing climate.

A word should be said about the climate . . . 'the proximity of the ocean cools the air in summer and modifies the cold in winter. It is, in short, a dry bracing atmosphere, stimulating to the senses and strengthening to the system'.

An early morning walk on the Buchan coast was certainly a stimulating experience.

After such a hopeful beginning to their venture it was a crushing blow to the GNSR directors to find that the hotel, instead of being a great asset, was a financial liability. The tourist season was far too shart to be profitable and the hotel was always run at a loss. During the war, it was requisitioned for military purposes and afterwards, when it was partially destroyed by fire, a north-east man purchased the remains and had the building demolished in 1950. That was not quite the end of the story, however, because much of the stonework was carefully salvaged and transported to a site south of Stonehaven. There, the business man had his house built of the salvaged red granite and throughout the house, finely sculptured stonework and embellished arches of the Cruden Bay Hotel can still be seen.

Unlike the remainder of the Buchan line, the Boddam branch had a goods service which varied little during the year and over the years. During the life of the GNSR the service was one goods train up and down each day almost without exception. The fishing villages or Port Erroll and Boddam provided an essentially local fishing industry and so the great fish train specials of Peterhead and Fraserburgh were almost unknown on the branch. The passenger trains were occasionally run 'mixed' to cope with the like of the sales at Ellon.

As it was a tourist line, the Great North took great pains to provide a fast and efficient service for its passengers. In 1898, the year when many services were reduced, the Company put on new accelerated services for Cruden Bay and these were, considering the nature of the line, quite

The first train to leave Boddam Station on the opening of the Ellon to Boddam branch was on 2nd August 1897. GNSR Class 'G10', No. 86, one of ten specially built for the Aberdeen to Dyce and the Aberdeen to Culter suburban services, is seen at Boddam on this first train.

G.N.S.R.A. Collection

fast. In a brochure for 1901, the following times were given:

> 'By the West Coast route, a train leaves Euston at 8 p.m. and is due in Aberdeen at 7.15 a.m. the next morning. A train in connection leaves Aberdeen at 8.10 a.m. and reaches Cruden Bay at 9.25 a.m. . . . . By the East Coast route, several fast trains are also run. The 8.15 p.m. from King's Cross, due Aberdeen at 7.20 a.m. makes the same connection.

In comparing these runs with modern day timings they are, relatively speaking, just as good.

Although the branch was given an excellent service and had adequate facilities, it never paid in quite the way the Great North's directors had hoped. The LNER closed the line to passengers on 31st October 1932, initially for the winter months only, but the service was never resumed. In 1945 the line was completely closed to all traffic but the stations still dealt with parcels and miscellaneous passenger train traffic. Finally, in 1950, the rails were lifted and thus closed one of the chapters of the GNSR history, a chapter, albeit short, but one of the most colourful and in a way the most disappointing. Little remains today, but for the energetic enthusiast the course of most of the line may still be trodden by foot.

Lying three miles north of Boddam, Peterhead was the object of railway promoters as early as 1846, but it was not until 1856, with the appearance of the rural schemes, that the building of the line seemed possible. The two schemes were put forward respectively by a Sir Alexander Anderson and a Mr John Duncan. After a protracted contest Sir Alexander Anderson's scheme was adopted and under it was formed the Buchan and Formartine section of the Great North.

The line of the railway projected by Mr Duncan started from Waterloo Station, and, passing over the Old Town Links, crossed the Don just below the new (road) bridge whence it followed the coast closely as far as Newburgh. There it left the coast and, striking almost due north, passed through the village of Ellon and continued nearly in the route of the present line as far as Auchnagatt. At that point, it diverged to the east and, passing through Crichie, again joined the route of the present line at Aden and followed it, more or less closely, to Peterhead. There was also to be a line to Fraserburgh starting from the vicinity of Pitfour.

In 1861, the section from Dyce to Mintlaw was opened and, sufficient capital now having been raised, Peterhead was reached in 1862. Mintlaw was originally to have been the Peterhead/Fraserburgh junction but in 1863 an Act was passed whereby Maud was made the junction. From Maud, the line follows an easy course along the banks of the Ugie and, approaching Mintlaw, it passes close to the site of Deer Abbey. It is possible to trace the founding at the beginning of the thirteenth century of the Abbey of St. Mary of Deer, which has a long and chequered history, not always creditable. There is no record of its having been inhabited at a later period than the sixteenth century. Extensive gardens adjoin the site which slopes to the south

10

Maud Junction, 1910. A typical Buchan line train of the period heads south towards Aberdeen, behind a Kitson-built 4-4-0, whilst another 4-4-0 simmers in the goods yard waiting to take a 'cattle special' south.

British Railways

and which probably, like the site of Westminster Abbey, had been a swamp, the better to offer security to the monk and sanctuary for the people.

Passing Mintlaw, the line reaches Longside where a branch to carry supplies was laid for about three and a half miles to the south to Lenabo Airship Station which was established in 1915 by the Admiralty. Sold to the Government to work this branch were the GNSR's 0-4-0Ts, Nos. 13 and 14 which were sent to England when the branch was uplifted after the 1914-18 War. One of these was not withdrawn until 1943 and probably had the distinction of being one of the oldest working locomotives of the GNSR at that time.

The main line continues past the remains of the castles of Ravens Craig and Inverugie and finally runs into Peterhead Station. There, another branch, seven and a half furlongs in length, ran round the north side of the town and down a final 1 in 70 gradient to the harbour. On the south side of the harbour was the terminus of a narrow gauge line, some three miles long, which ran up to the quarries where the famous Peterhead granite was hewn. The line was built for the construction of the south breakwater and had no physical connection with the Great North.

Peterhead was described in glowing terms in the adverts of the time and, for a line whose proceeds came mainly from goods traffic, the town had, to interest the traveller, a variety of amenities such as boating, fishing, golfing and the famous swimming and medicinal baths. Above all, Peterhead was famed for herring!

In the early 1880s, whale fishing had provided the income for the fishermen. Gradually whale fishing failed and soon herring was pouring out of Peterhead by the ton. In 1890, at £4 per ton to Billingsgate, the herring earned the 'sixpences' for the Great North. The 'fish specials' became a yearly event and the traffic sometimes assumed monumental proportions. The following extract from a weekly circular for July 1896 shows the importance of 'The Fish'.

Main Line and Buchan Sections
Extra Special Fish Trains

'It is probable that Extra Special Trains may be run at any time upon Main Line, Buchan and Macduff Sections with Fish Traffic, Empty Fish Trucks or Pilot Engines of which only Telegraphic Notices can be given.

It is of the utmost importance that all concerned should be on the alert to receive notices of such Trains, and to pass them without delay'.

Such methods of working occasionally led to trains being hurriedly sent out to meet the arrival of the fishing fleet only to discover that the ships had been delayed for twenty-four hours. Such losses, however, were more than offset by the receipts for the next consignment. The fish trains were run at speeds often greater than the passenger trains and, indeed, it often came about that 'the fish' was given priority over the passengers.

Trains for the harbour branch were usually worked twice a day with the engine propelling the wagons down to the harbour. The guard kept a look-out and gave the driver the signalling directions. The Peterhead agent had also to arrange for trains to work the Slaughterhouse Siding as and when required.

As previously noted, Buchan had been the object of railway promoters as early as 1846 with the proposed Great North of Scotland (Eastern Extension) Railway. This was to be a line to Fraserburgh from Dyce with a branch from Stewartfield to Peterhead. However, this fell through and it was left to the Formartine and Buchan, in 1858, to put forward the plan for the line as it now exists today. Construction was started from Dyce and in July 1861 Mintlaw was reached. Originally Mintlaw was to be the junction for Fraserburgh, but in 1863 an Act was passed abandoning the branch from Mintlaw to Fraserburgh and authorizing the line from Maud by way of Strichen and Lonmay. Fraserburgh was finally reached in April 1865. In 1866 the Formartine and Buchan, to which the Great North had subscribed a considerable sum towards the construction, was amalgamated with the GNSR.

Because the Buchan line 'cuts across the grain' of the countryside with its river valleys, the gradients are, of necessity, quite steep. Leaving Dyce, the railway drops at first at 1 in 85 but after crossing the Don, the line climbs at

1 in 105. Almost a mile beyond Newmachar through the cutting, a final 1 in 75 brings the line to the summit. It is now a gradual descent until, crossing the Ythan on a four-arched stone viaduct, Ellon is reached. The railway climbs gradually passed Auchnagatt then drops at 1 in 100 to Maud Junction. At the south end, the line divides and it is here that the passenger trains halted to be split. On the west side of the station was the turntable and there are four platforms, not all in use now; two on the Peterhead line and two on the Fraserburgh. Maud was developed as quite an important agricultural and livestock centre. In addition to the normal station buildings there is a small restaurant where the traveller may enjoy a wholesome meal at a modest price.

Leaving Maud, the line climbs and falls past Brucklay, climbs again and finally drops into Strichen at 1 in 66. There is now a gradual climb to Mormond Halt where, in the side of Mormond Hill, the figure of a stag has been cut out of the turf and filled in with white stones. This white stag can be seen for miles around. From Mormond, the line drops at 1 in 70/80 to Lonmay, levels out slightly through Rathen and from beyond there, through Philorth to Fraserburgh (47¼) continues, more or less, level.

For almost the whole of its length the Buchan line was single but in 1920 a section of the line from Parkhill to a new cabin at Elrick (about 1 mile) was doubled. It was not long however, with the reduction of excess wartime traffic, that this was seen to be an uneconomic proposition. Thus in September 1924, the line was reduced to single track and Elrick cabin was closed.

As can be seen from the special circular, Philorth Station was the private station of Lord Saltoun. No doubt the agent in charge could never complain about being inundated with passengers. In addition to his own station, Lord Saltoun had his own private mail-bag and the following is an extract from Working of Guards, Carriages and Mails, 1st November 1895:

Only one other branch remains to be described and this is the St. Combs line, the last to be built by the Great North. With the passing of the Light Railways Act in 1896 which enabled the railways to be built and operated cheaply (theoretically at any rate!), the Great North decided to construct a light railway connecting St. Combs (5¼ miles) with Inverallochy and Fraserburgh. Although this matter has been the subject of much contention and discussion, space does not permit giving details in this article. The line was duly opened on 1st July 1903. Apart from St. Combs and Cairnbulg there were the provisional halts of Kirkton Bridge and Philorth Bridge. Although the original timetable showed Inverallochy, this was soon changed to Cairnbulg. The following is a copy of the original timetable with some notes from the weekly circular for 3rd July 1903.

Down Trains

Stations	Pass. a.m.	Pass. a.m.	Mixed a.m.	Pass. p.m.	Pass. p.m.	Mixed p.m.
Fraserburgh, depart	6.30	8.00	10.30	1.00	3.40	6.40
Inverallochy	6.42	8.12	10.42	1.12	3.52	6.52
St. Combs, arrive	6.47	8.17	10.47	1.17	3.57	6.57

Up Trains

Stations	Mixed a.m.	Mixed a.m.	Mixed a.m.	Pass. a.m.	Mixed p.m.	Pass. p.m.
St. Combs, depart	7.00	8.45	11.45	2.45	5.30	7.15
Inverallochy	7.06	8.51	11.51	2.51	5.36	7.21
Fraserburgh, arrive	7.17	9.02	12.02	3.02	5.47	7.52

There is no telegraph or telephonic communication on the Railway. No train or engine must run upon the Railway at a rate of speed exceeding at any time 25 miles an hour, or, when passing the level crossing at Inverallochy Station, at a rate of speed exceeding 10 miles an hour.

Staff
Mr William Gordon, Agent, St. Combs : Mr Hans Hardie, Agent, Inverallochy

It was not long however before the timetable was altered to include two extra Saturdays only passengers and one Wednesday only passenger, up and down. Obviously there was not enough room for the fish workers and their creels in the one train! All engines working on this branch had to be fitted with 'cow-catchers', of course, and this gave the engines a unique appearance.

A GNSR 0-6-0 stands at St. Combs Station in early LNER days.

A. Sangster Collection

The Buchan branches were the first in the north-east of Scotland to receive their closure notices under the 1962 Transport Act, and Beeching's axe fell on the passenger services to Peterhead and St. Combs in May 1965. The Fraserburgh service lingered on until October 1965 and the remaining freight services were withdrawn a few years later, Peterhead in 1970 and Fraserburgh in 1979. St. Combs had already been closed to freight some time before withdrawal of the passenger services. So ended over a century of service to the Aberdeenshire community.

ST. COMBS LIGHT RAILWAY.

		M O													Sats only.
		A.M.	A M	A.M.		A.M.	P.M.	P M		P.M.	P M			P.M.
FRASERBRO'	de	5 0	6 5	8 5	.	10 30	1 15	2 55	...	4 40	6 50	..	10 15
Cairnbulg		5 14	6 19	8 19	...	10 44	1 29	3 9	...	4 54	7 4	...	10 29
ST. COMBS	arr.	5 20	6 25	8 25	..	10 50	1 35	3 15	...	5 0	7 10	...	10 35

		M O													Sats only.
		A.M.	A.M.	A.M.		A.M.	P M.	P.M.		P.M.	P. M.			P.M.
ST. COMBS	de	5 30	6 38	8 35	...	11 40	2 20	4 0	..	5 40	7 20	...	10 43
Cairnbulg		5 32	6 40	8 42	...	11 47	2 27	4 7	...	5 47	7 27	...	10 50
FRASERBRO'	arr.	5 50	6 53	8 55	..	12 0	2 40	4 20	...	6 0	7 40	...	11 8

Formartine and Buchan Section.

Up Trains. (Will not depart from)

		A.M.	A.M.	A.M.
	Invergordon, per I. & A., *depart*	—	—	7 50
	Inverness	—	6 40	10 5
	Dufftown	—	9 15	12 10
	Keith	—	7 0	10 5 1 0
	Banff, per B. P. & S.	—	9 15	12 20
	Portsoy, per do.	—	9 27	12 25
	Banff and Macduff	6 50	10 0	12 10
	Oldmeldrum	8 24	11 30	2 15
	Alford	7 40	10 45	—

Down Trains. Will not depart from

Miles		1 Goods	2 Mixed 1 and 3	3 Mixed Parl. 1 and 3	4 Mixed 1 and 3	5 Mixed 1 and 3
	MAIN LINE	A.M.	A.M.	P.M.	P.M.	P.M.
	Aberdeen, depart	5 0	8 50	1 40	3 20	6 0
1¼	Kittybrewster	5 10	8 58	1 48	3 28	6 8
2½	Woodside		9 1	1 52	3 31	6 12
4¼	Buxburn	5 23	9 7	1 57	3 36	6 18
	Dyce Junction *arr.*	5 30	9 13	2 3	3 42	6 24
	FORMARTINE & BUCHAN					
6½	Dyce Junction *depart*	5 38	9 16	2 5	3 43	6 25
7½	Parkhill	5 44	9 20	2 10	3 47	6 29
11½	Newmachar	6 5	9 33	2 28	3 59	6 44
14¾	Udny	6 20	9 45	2 40	4 9	6 55
16½	Logierieve		9 50	2 45	4 13	7 0
18	Esslemont	6 35	9 55	2 51	4 18	7 5
19¾	Ellon arrive	6 45	—	—	4 25	—
	Ellon depart		10 2	3 0		7 12
23¼	Arnage		10 12	3 11		7 25
27¼	Auchnagatt		10 24	3 24		7 37
31¼	Brucklay		10 39	3 39		7 50
35¼	Old Deer & Mintlaw		10 50	3 51		8 4
38¾	Longside		11 0	4 1		8 14
41	New Seat		11 6	4 7		8 19
42½	Inverugie		11 12	4 13		8 25
44½	Peterhead *arrive*		11 20	4 20		8 35

Up Trains. Will not depart from

Miles		1 Mixed 1 and 3	2 Mixed 1 and 3	3 Mixed Parl. 1 and 3	4 Goods	5 Mixed 1 and 3
	FORMARTINE & BUCHAN.	A.M.	A.M.	A.M.	P.M.	P.M.
	Peterhead *before*	—	7 35	11 40	—	5 20
2	Inverugie	—	7 41	11 46	—	5 25
3¾	New Seat	—	7 47	11 52	—	5 32
5¾	Longside	—	7 56	12 0	—	5 40
9	Old Deer & Mintlaw	—	8 9	12 10	—	5 50
13	Brucklay	—	8 20	12 20	—	6 2
17½	Auchnagatt	—	8 35	12 35	—	6 16
21¼	Arnage	—	8 48	12 46	—	6 27
24¾	Ellon	7 0	9 0	12 58	4 45	6 39
26¼	Esslemont	7 7	9 7	1 3	—	6 44
28	Logierieve	7 13	9 12	1 8	—	6 49
29¾	Udny	7 20	9 17	1 13	5 0	6 55
32½	Newmachar	7 30	9 33	1 23	5 12	7 5
36¾	Parkhill	7 43	9 44	1 34	—	7 16
	Dyce Junction	7 47	9 48	1 38	5 26	7 20
	MAIN LINE.					
38	Dyce Junction *dep.*	7 50	9 49	1 40	5 28	7 22
40	Buxburn	8 0	9 54	1 47	—	7 29
41¾	Woodside	8 4	9 58	1 51	—	7 35
42¾	Kittybrewster	8 12	10 5	2 0	5 40	7 40
44¼	Aberdeen, arrive	8 20	10 15	2 10	5 50	7 50

Down Trains

	1	2	3	4	5
Alford arrive	10 5	—	—	—	9 10
Oldmeldrum	9 25	—	—	—	8 25
Banff and Macduff	11 10	—	4 0	—	9 50
Portsoy, per B. P. & S.	11 40	—	—	—	—
Banff, per do.	11 50	—	—	—	—
Keith	10 51	—	3 57	—	9 50
Dufftown	11 40	—	4 45	—	—
Inverness, per I. & A.	1 45	—	7 0	—	—
Invergordon	5 45	—	9 5	—	—

1907

BUCHAN SECTION Passenger Trains.

FROM ABERDEEN

	A.M.	A.M.	A.M.		P.M.	P.M.	P.M.	Sats only	P.M.	P.M.
AB'DEEN	6 55	8 10	9 35	12 40	1 30	4 5			4 37	7 0
K'brewster	6 59	8 14	9 39	12 44	1 35	4 10				7 5
Woodside	7 3		9 43	12 48		A				7 9
Buckaburn	7 7		9 47	12 52		A				7 13
Dyce Jun.	7 13	8 23	9 54	12 58	1 44	4 21				7 20
Parkhill	7 16			1 1		4 25				7 23
Newmachar	7 26			1 12	1 54	4 37				7 34
Udny	7 33	8 38	10 11	1 20	2 1	4 48				7 41
Logierieve	7 37		10 15	1 24		4 52				7 45
Esslemont	7 41			1 28		4 56				7 49
Ellon	7 47	8 47	10 22	1 34	2 8	5 0	5 11			7 54
Arnage	7 56		10 31	1 43		Stop	5 20			7 19
Auchnagatt	8 6	9 3	10 41	1 55			5 30			8 17
Maud Jun.	8 14	9 10	10 48	2 3			5 37			8 24
Maud Jun.	8 23	9 15	10 53	2 9			5 42			8 30
Brucklay	8 28		10 57	2 14			5 48			8 34
Strichen	8 36	9 26	11 5	2 22			5 55			8 42
Mormond	8 42		11 11	2 28			6 1			8 48
Lonmay	8 48	9 37	11 16	2 34			6 8			8 54
Rathen	8 54	9 43	11 22	2 40			6 13			9 0
F'BURGH	9 2	9 50	11 30	2 50			6 21			9 10
Maud Jun.	8 20	9 20	10 53	2 9			5 42			8 30
Mintlaw	8 27	9 30	11 0	2 17			5 50			8 36
Longside	8 35	9 44	11 7	2 24			6 2			8 45
Newseat	8 40		11 12	2 29			6 7			8 50
Invurgie	8 45		11 17	2 34			6 7	8 55		9 4
PETERH'D	8 50	9 55	11 22	2 40			6 12	9 10		9 10

TO ABERDEEN

	B A.M.	B A.M.	C P.M.		D P.M.	E P.M.	Sats only P.M.	Mixed Mond P.M.
PETERH'D	7 40	9 30	1 5	3 40	5 47			7 5
Inverugie	7 45	9 35	1 10	3 44				7 11
Newseat	7 49	9 39	1 14	3 48				7 16
Longside	7 55	9 44	1 20	3 53				7 23
Mintlaw	8 4	9 54	1 29	4 2	6 5			7 34
Maud Jun.	8 12	10 2	1 37	4 10	6 12			7 45
F'BURGH	7 30	9 25	12 55	3 35	5 37			7 0
Rathen	7 37	9 31	1 2	3 41				7 7
Lonmay	7 43	9 37	1 8	3 46				7 13
Mormond	7 50	9 43	1 15					7 19
Strichen	7 56	9 49	1 21	3 58	5 55			7 26
Brucklay	8 7	10 0	1 32		6 5			7 37
Maud Jun.	8 11	10 5	1 37	4 10	6 10			7 42
Maud Jun.	8 20	10 11	1 44	4 15	6 18			7 50
Auchnagatt	8 30	10 21	1 55	4 23				8 0
Arnage	8 38	10 31	2 3					8 7
Ellon	8 50	10 40	2 12	4 37	6 38	7 55		8 16
Esslemont	8 10	10 45	2 17					8 21
Logierieve	8 15	10 49	2 21					8 25
Udny	8 21	10 54	2 27	4 48	6 49	8 6		8 31
Newmachar	8 30	11 2		4 57	6 58	8 15		8 40
Parkhill	8 41	11 10	2 45					8 47
Dyce Jun.	8 45	9 18	11 15	2 50	5 5		8 23	8 51
Buckaburn	8 51			2 55				8 56
Woodside	8 55			3 0				9 0
K'brewster	8 59	9 27	11 24	3 10	5 14	7 15	8 32	9 4
AB'DEEN	9 5	9 33	11 30	3 15	5 20	7 21	8 38	9 10

A Stop at Woodside and Buckburn for passengers for Buchan section on timeous notice being given to the Stationmaster.
B Passengers from the Buchan Section for Dinside and beyond travel to Aberdeen to join the 10·10 a.m. Train.
C Passengers from the Buchan Section for Insch and beyond travel to Aberdeen to join the 2·20 p.m. Train.
D Passengers from the Buchan Section for beyond directly travel to Aberdeen to join the 4·45 p.m. Train.
E During July and August only

1907

BUCHAN SECTION—Goods Trains.

FROM ABERDEEN.

									B Engine only.	B Engine only
		A.M.	A.M.		A.M		A.M		P.M.	P.M.
KITTYBREWSTER	dep	4 55	5 15		5 45		11 20			
Bucksburn							11 40			
Dyce		5 25	5 45		6 10		12/10			
Parkhill					6 20					
Newmachar					6 42		12 32			
Udny					6 59		12 50			
Logierieve					7 8		1 0			
Esslemont					7 18		1 10			
Ellon					7 25		1 45	5 30		
Arnage			6 42				2 3			
Auchnagatt		6 30					2 20			
Maud	arr	6 41	7 5				2 35			
Maud	dep	6 51					3 25			7 45
Brucklay		7 3					3 37			
Strichen		7 22					3 58			
Mormond		7 33					4 9			
Lonmay		7 47					4 20			
Rathen		7 58					4 30			
FRASERBURGH	arr	8 10					4 40			8 20
Maud	dep		7 20				3 20			
Mintlaw			7 39				3 37	6 5		
Longside			7 55			For Cruden Section.	3 53			
Inverugie			8 7				4 10			
PETERHEAD	arr		8 15				4 20	6 25		

B July and August only

TO ABERDEEN.

				Engine only						C Engine only
		A.M.		A.M.	A.M.	P.M		P.M.	P.M.	P.M.
PETERHEAD	dep	8 15		11 35		2 0				
Inverugie		8 25								
Longside		8 43				2 24				
Mintlaw		9 0				2 41				
Maud	arr	9 11		12 0		2 52				
FRASERBURGH	dep	7 0		Stop	From Cruden Section			1 40	6 30	
Rathen		7 13						1 51		
Lonmay		7 57						2 3		
Mormond		8 10								
Strichen		8 36						2 27		
Brucklay		8 55						2 47		
Maud	arr	9 3						2 54	7 20	
Maud	dep	9 30				3 5		3 18	8 5	
Auchnagatt		9 48						3 33	8 17	
Arnage		10 5						3 47		
Ellon		10 55			11 50			4 4	8 46	5 20
Esslemont					12 0			4 14		
Logierieve					12/10			4 24		
Udny					12 50			5 5		
Newmachar					1 12			5 25		
Parkhill					1 32					
Dyce		12 0			1 47	4 18		5 44	9 25	5 51
Kittybrewster		12 21			2 11	4 39		6 4	9 47	6 0
ABERDEEN	arr	12 27			2 17	4 45		6 10	9 53	Stop

GREAT NORTH OF SCOTLAND RAILWAY.

Buchan Section.

TRAIN.	First	Comp	Third	Brake Third.	Pass. Van.	FROM	TO	FOR
A.M.								
6·50 Daily			1	1	1	Aberdeen	Peterhead	9·30 a.m.
,, Except Saturdays			1			Maud	,,	3·40 p.m.—9·30 a.m. Weds.
,, Daily			1		1	Aberdeen	Fraserburgh	9·25 a.m.
,, Mondays				1		,,	,,	9·25 a.m.
8·10 Daily		1				,,	Peterhead	7·15 a.m.—1·5 Fris. and Sats.
,, Daily			1			,,	,,	1·5 p.m.
,, Daily					1	,,	,,	7·5 p.m. Goods portion.
,, Daily		1	1		1	,,	Fraserburgh	12·55 p.m.
,, Mondays (Milk Cans)					1	,,	Udny	9·30 a.m. on Mondays.
9·35 Daily			1	1	1	,,	Peterhead	1·5 p.m.
,, Mondays and Saturdays			1			,,	,,	Home.
,, Daily			1		1	,,	Fraserburgh	12·55 p.m. (Empty).
P.M.								
12·40 Daily			1	1	1	,,	Peterhead	3·40 p.m.
,, Saturdays			1			,,	,,	3·40 p.m.
,, Wednesdays			2			Maud	,,	3·40 p.m.
,, Daily			1	1	1	Aberdeen	Fraserburgh	3·35 p.m.
4·27 Daily		1	2		1	,,	Peterhead	7·5 p.m.—less 1 Third.
,, Fridays			2			,,	,,	Home.
,, Fridays			1			,,	,,	7·15 a.m. on Mondays.
,, Saturdays			1			,,	,,	Home.
,, Daily		1	1		1	,,	Fraserburgh	7·0 p.m.
,, Daily (Milk Cans)					1	,,	Udny	9·30 a.m.—3·15 a.m. on Mons.
7·0 Daily		1	2		1	,,	Peterhead	7·15 a.m.
,, Fridays			1			,,	,,	7·15 a.m.
,, Saturdays			1			,,	,,	7·15 a.m.
,, Daily		1	1		1	,,	Fraserburgh	7·5 a.m.
A.M.								
7·15 Daily		1	2		1	Peterhead	Aberdeen	4·27 p.m.
,, Except Saturdays		1				,,	,,	8·10 a.m.
,, Fridays and Saturdays			2			,,	,,	4·27 p.m.
,, Mondays			1			,,	,,	Home.
7·5 Daily			1	1	1	Fraserburgh	,,	4·27 p.m.
9·30 Daily		1	1		1	Peterhead	,,	12·40 p.m.
,, Saturdays			1			,,	,,	12·40 p.m.
,, Wednesdays			2			,,	Maud	12·40 p.m.
9·25 Daily		1	1		1	Fraserburgh	Aberdeen	12·40 p.m.
9·30 Daily (Milk)					1	Udny	,,	4·27 p.m.
P.M.								
1·5 Daily			1	1	1	Peterhead	,,	9·35 a.m.
,, Daily			1			,,	,,	8·10 a.m.
,, Fridays and Saturdays		1				,,	,,	8·10 a.m.
12·55 Daily			1	1	1	Fraserburgh	,,	8·10 a.m.
,, Daily (Empty)		1			1	,,	,,	9·35 a.m.
3·40 Daily		1	2		1	Peterhead	,,	7·0 p.m.
,, Fridays and Saturdays			1			,,	,,	7·0 p.m.
,, Except Fris. and Sats.			1			,,	Maud	6·50 a.m.
3·35 Daily		1	1		1	Fraserburgh	Aberdeen	7·0 p.m.
7·5 Daily		1	1		1	Peterhead	,,	6·50 a.m.
,, Saturdays			1			,,	Maud	6·50 a.m. on Mondays.
,, Daily					1	,,	,,	6·30 a.m. Goods to Aberdeen.
7·0 Daily					1	Fraserburgh	Aberdeen	6·50 a.m.
,, Saturdays			1			,,	,,	6·50 a.m. on Mondays.

MAUD AND FRASERBURGH SECTION.

In addition to the Through Carriages, the following extra carriages will also be run between Maud and Fraserburgh, viz. :—

Train.	DOWN TRAINS.	Vehicles.	Train.	UP TRAINS.	Vehicles.
A.M.			**A.M.**		
8·20	Except Mondays,	1 Third.	7·5	Mondays,	1 Brake.
8·20	Mondays,	1 Brake.	9·25	Daily,	1 do.
10·53	Daily,	1 do.	9·25	Wednesdays,	2 Thirds.
P.M.			**P.M.**		
2·9	Wednesdays	2 Thirds.	12·55	Wednesdays and Saturdays,	1 Brake.
2·9	Wednesdays and Saturdays,	1 Brake.	3·35	Wednesdays and Saturdays,	1 do.
5·50	Wednesdays and Saturdays,	1 do.	7·0	Except Saturdays,	1 Third.
8·30	Saturdays,	1 do.	7·0	Saturdays,	1 Brake.

Brake Third may be sent from Fraserburgh by any Train when required. Maud to return it by next Train.

CRUDEN SECTION Trains to be 0·1·1·0·1—Certain Trains on Mondays and Saturdays to have an extra Third if required.

ST. COMBS BRANCH Trains to be 2 Thirds and Van, and extra Thirds as required.

Station received at.		PARTICULARS OF MAILS. L=Letter Bags. P=Parcel Bags. X=Private Bags.

CRUDEN SECTION.

7·35 a.m. Down Goods Train.

See 5·40 a.m. Down Buchan Goods Train.

8·55 a.m. Down Train.

Ellon . .	L	Aberdeen to Hatton and Port-Errol (Cruden Bay).
Do. .	X	Aberdeen to Cruden Bay Hotel.
Do. .	L	Cal. T.P.O. to Hatton, Port-Erroll (Cruden Bay), and *e*Boddam.

10·25 a.m. Down Train *(Mondays only)*.

| Ellon . . | L | *m*Aberdeen to Boddam. |
| Do. . | L | *m*Cal. T.P.O. to Boddam. |

5·23 p.m. Down Train.

| Ellon . . | L | Aberdeen to Hatton and Port-Erroll (Cruden Bay). |
| Do. . | X | Aberdeen to Cruden Bay Hotel. |

7·40 a.m. Up Train.

Cruden Bay	L	Port-Erroll to Aberdeen.
Do. .	X	Cruden Bay Hotel to Aberdeen.
Hatton .	L	Hatton to Aberdeen.

12·50 p.m. Up Train.

| Longhaven | L | Longhaven to Aberdeen. |

3·55 p.m. Up Train.

Boddam .	L	Boddam to Aberdeen.
Cruden Bay	L	Port-Erroll to Aberdeen.
Do. .	P	Port-Erroll to Aberdeen.
Do. .	X	*w*Cruden Bay Hotel to Aberdeen.
Hatton .	L	Hatton to Aberdeen.
Do. .	P	Hatton to Aberdeen.

7·15 p.m. Up Train.

| Cruden Bay | X | *y*Cruden Bay Hotel to Aberdeen. |

ST. COMBS BRANCH.

3·10 p.m. Down Train.

| Fraserburgh | L | Fraserburgh to Inverallochy (Cairnbulg), and St. Combs. |

Great North of Scotland Railway.
LUGGAGE.
BODDAM
From...............

Great North of Scotland Railway.
LUGGAGE.
CRUDEN BAY
From...............

Station received at.		PARTICULARS OF MAILS. L = Letter Bags. P = Parcel Bags. X = Private Bags.

Buchan Section—*Continued.*

7·5 and 7·15 a.m. Up Trains.

Ellon	L	Port-Erroll and Hatton to Aberdeen.
Do.	X	Cruden Bay Hotel to Aberdeen.
Udny	L	Udny Station, Udny, Methlick, and Tarves to Aberdeen.
Do.	X	Haddo House to Aberdeen.
Newmachar	L	Newmachar to Aberdeen.

9·25 and 9·30 a.m. Up Trains.

Fraserburgh	L	Fraserburgh to Aberdeen, Edinburgh, and Glasgow.
Peterhead	L	Peterhead to Aberdeen, Perth, Edinburgh, and Glasgow.
Do.	P	Peterhead to Aberdeen.
Auchnagatt	L	Auchnagatt to Aberdeen.
Ellon	L	Ellon and Newburgh to Aberdeen.

12·55 and 1·5 p.m. Up Trains

Fraserburgh	L	Fraserburgh to Aberdeen and Cal. T.P.O.
Do.	P	Fraserburgh to Aberdeen.
Rathen	L	Rathen to Aberdeen.
Strichen	L	Strichen to Aberdeen and Cal. T.P.O.
Peterhead	L	Peterhead to Aberdeen and Cal. T.P.O.
Do.	P	Peterhead to Aberdeen.
Longside	L	Longside to Aberdeen and Cal. T.P.O.
Mintlaw	L	Mintlaw to Aberdeen and Cal. T.P.O.
Maud	L	Maud to Aberdeen Station.
Auchnagatt	L	Auchnagatt to Aberdeen.
Ellon	L	Longhaven to Aberdeen.
Bucksburn	L	Bucksburn to Aberdeen.
Wooaside	L	Woodside to Aberdeen and Cal. T.P.O.

3·35 and 3·40 p.m. Up Trains.

Fraserburgh	L	Fraserburgh to Peterhead, Aberdeen, and Cal. T.P.O.
Do.	P	Fraserburgh to Aberdeen.
Lonmay	L	Lonmay to Aberdeen.
Do.	P	Lonmay to Aberdeen.
Peterhead	L	Peterhead to Fraserburgh, Aberdeen, and Cal. T.P.O.
Do.	P	Peterhead to Aberdeen.
Longside	L	Longside to Aberdeen and Cal. T.P.O.
Do.	P	Longside to Aberdeen.
Mintlaw	L	Mintlaw to Aberdeen.
Do.	P	Mintlaw to Aberdeen.
Maud	L	Maud to Aberdeen.
Do.	P	Maud to Aberdeen.
Ellon	L	Ellon, Boddam. Port-Erroll, and Hatton to Aberdeen.
Do.	X	wCruden Bay Hotel to Aberdeen.
Do.	P	Ellon, Port-Erroll, and Hatton to Aberdeen.
Udny	L	Udny Station, Udny, Methlick, and Tarves to Aberdeen.
Do.	X	Haddo House and Mains of Haddo to Aberdeen.
Do.	P	Methlick and Tarves to Aberdeen.
Newmachar	L	Newmachar and Whitecairns to Aberdeen.

7·0 and 7·5 p.m. Up Trains.

Fraserburgh	L	Fraserburgh to Rathen, Lonmay, Strichen, and Aberdeen.
Do.	P	Fraserburgh to Aberdeen.
Rathen	L	Rathen to Aberdeen.
Do.	P	Rathen to Aberdeen.
Lonmay	L	Lonmay to Aberdeen.
Strichen	L	Strichen to Aberdeen.
Do.	P	Strichen to Aberdeen.
Peterhead	L	Peterhead to Longside, Mintlaw, Maud, and Aberdeen.
Do.	P	Peterhead to Aberdeen.
Longside	L	Longside to Aberdeen.
Mintlaw	L	Mintlaw to Aberdeen.
Do.	P	Mintlaw to Aberdeen.
Maud	L	Maud to Aberdeen Station.
Do.	P	Maud to Aberdeen.
Ellon	L	Ellon to Aberdeen.
Do.	P	Ellon to Aberdeen.
Do.	X	yCruden Bay Hotel to Aberdeen—*To be put off at Schoolhill for delivery at Post Office by Station Staff.*

Station received at.		PARTICULARS OF MAILS. L = Letter Bags. P = Parcel Bags. X = Private Bags.

BUCHAN SECTION.

4·55 a.m. Down Goods Train.

K'brewster	L	Aberdeen to Auchnagatt, Maud, Strichen, Lonmay, Rathen, and Fraserburgh (2).
Do.	P	Aberdeen to Maud, Strichen, and Fraserburgh.
Do.	L	eCal. T.P.O. to Auchnagatt, Maud, Strichen, Lonmay, Rathen, and Fraserburgh.
Do.	L	eGlasgow to Fraserburgh.
Do.	P	eGlasgow and ePerth to Fraserburgh.
Do.	L	ePerth to Maud, Strichen, and Fraserburgh.
Strichen	L	Strichen to Fraserburgh.
Lonmay	L	Lonmay to Fraserburgh.

5·15 a.m. Down Goods Train.

K'brewster	L	Aberdeen to Ellon, Newburgh (Ellon), Mintlaw, Longside, and Peterhead (2).
Do.	P	Aberdeen to Ellon, Mintlaw, Longside, and Peterhead.
Do.	L	eCal. T.P.O. to Ellon, Newburgh (Ellon), Mintlaw, Longside, and Peterhead.
Do.	L	eEdinburgh and eGlasgow to Peterhead.
Do.	P	eGlasgow and ePerth to Peterhead.
Do.	L	ePerth to Ellon, Mintlaw, and Peterhead.
Maud	L	Maud to Peterhead.
Mintlaw	L	Mintlaw to Peterhead.
Longside	L	Longside to Peterhead.

5·40 a.m. Down Goods Train.

| Dyce | L | Aberdeen to Udny, Longhaven, and eBoddam. |

6·50 a.m. Down Train.

Aberdeen	L	Aberdeen to Dyce, Newmachar, Udny, Tarves (Udny), and Methlick (Udny).
Do.	X	Aberdeen to Haddo House (Udny) and Mains of Haddo (Udny).
Do.	P	Aberdeen to Dyce.

8·10 a.m. Down Train.

Aberdeen	L	Aberdeen to Hatton, Port-Erroll (Cruden Bay), Fraserburgh, and Peterhead.
Do.	X	Aberdeen to Cruden Bay Hotel.
Do.	L	Cal. T.P.O. to Hatton, Port-Erroll (Cruden Bay), eBoddam, Strichen, Lonmay, Fraserburgh, Maud, Mintlaw, and Peterhead.
Do.	L	Edinburgh to Fraserburgh and Peterhead.
Do.	L	eLondon to Fraserburgh and Peterhead.
Do.	P	Aberdeen to Port-Erroll (Cruden Bay).

9·35 a.m. Down Train.

| Aberdeen | L | Aberdeen to Dyce, Ellon, and mBoddam. |
| Do. | L | Cal. T.P.O. to Dyce, Ellon, and mBoddam. |

12·40 p.m. Down Train.

| Aberdeen | L | Aberdeen to Auchnagatt and Longside. |
| Do. | P | Aberdeen to Longside. |

4·27 p.m. Down Train.

| Aberdeen | L | Aberdeen to Newmachar, Whitecairns (Newmachar), Udny Station, and Methlick (Udny). |
| Do. | X | Aberdeen to Haddo House (Udny). |

4·27 p.m. Down Train—Contd.

Aberdeen	L	Aberdeen to Ellon, Hatton, Port-Erroll (Cruden Bay), Strichen, Lonmay, Rathen, Fraserburgh, Maud, Mintlaw, Longside, and Peterhead.
Do.	X	Aberdeen to Cruden Bay Hotel.
Do.	P	Aberdeen to Ellon, Maud, Strichen, Fraserburgh, Mintlaw, Longside, and Peterhead.
Maud	L	Fraserburgh to Peterhead.
Do.	L	Peterhead to Fraserburgh.

7·0 p.m. Down Train.

| Aberdeen | L | mAberdeen to Peterhead. |

GREAT NORTH OF SCOTLAND RAILWAY.
3.—BUCHAN SECTION.

Trains. / Guards.

Down	Up	NAME	FROM	TO
A.M.	A.M.			
4 55	...	A. Watson,	K'brewster,	Fraserburgh
...	9 25	Do.	Fraserburgh	Arnage.
9 35	P.M.	Do.	Arnage	Peterhead.
...	1 5	Do.	Peterhead	Aberdeen.
	A.M.			
5§15	...	B. Stuart,	K'brewster,	Peterhead.
...	8§15	Do.	Peterhead,	Aberdeen.
5 40	...	J. Thomson,	K'brewster,	Boddam.
...	9 55	Do.	Boddam,	Aberdeen.
6 50	...	W. Anderson,	Aberdeen,	Peterhead.
...	9 30	Do.	Peterhead,	Longside.
8 10	P.M.	Do.	Longside	Peterhead.
...	1 50	Do.	Peterhead,	Aberdeen.
8 10	...	J. Benzie,	Aberdeen,	Fraserburgh
P.M.	1 25	Do.	Fraserburgh	Aberdeen.
12 40	...	J. Grant,	Aberdeen,	Fraserburgh
...	6 30	Do.	Fraserburgh	Aberdeen.
10 20	...	Do.	Aberdeen,	K'brewster.
2 25	...	G. Milne,	Aberdeen,	Dyce.
...	3 3	Do.	Dyce,	Aberdeen.
4 27	...	*Do.	Aberdeen,	Peterhead.
...	7 5	Do.	Peterhead,	Aberdeen.
9 40	...	Do.	Aberdeen,	Inverurie, .
...	10 20	Do.	Inverurie,	K'brewster.
A.M.				
...	7 5	J. Florence,	Fraserburgh	Aberdeen.
11 20	...	Do.	K'brewster,	Fraserburgh
...	7 25	J. Reidford,	Fraserburgh	Maud.
10 53	P.M.	Do.	Maud,	Fraserburgh
P.M.	12 55	+Do.	Fraserburgh	Aberdeen.
4 27	...	Do.	Aberdeen,	Fraserburgb
...	12 55	J. Gilmore,	Fraserburgh	Maud.
2 9	...	Do.	Maud,	Fraserburgh
...	3 35	+Do.	Fraserburgh	Aberdeen.
7 0	...	Do.	Aberdeen,	Fraserburgh

See St. Combs Branch.

Down	Up	NAME	FROM	TO
...	1 5	A. Clark, 2nd,	Peterhead,	Maud.
12 40	...	Do.	Maud,	Peterhead.
...	3 40	Do.	Peterhead,	Aberdeen.
7 0	...	*Do.	Aberdeen,	Peterhead.

Trains. / Brakesmen.

Down	Up	NAME	FROM	TO
A.M.	A.M.			
4 55	...	c E. Cran,	K'brewster,	Lonmay.
...	7 25	Do.	Lonmay,	Maud.
9 20	...	Do. alone,	Maud,	Longside.
P.M.	9 30	g Do.	Longside,	Arnage.
1 20	P.M.	Do.	Aberdeen,	Inveramsay
...	2 30	Do.	Inveramsay.	K'brewster.
A.M.	A.M.			
3h55	...	J. Tocher,	Aberdeen,	K'brewster.
5§15	...	Do.	K'brewster,	Peterhead.
P.M.	8§15	Do.	Peterhead,	Aberdeen.
1 7		Do. alone,	Aberdeen,	K'brewster.
A.M.				
...	3h15	f W. Young,	Udny,	Aberdeen.
5 40	...	Do.	K'brewster,	Boddam.
...	9 55	Do.	Boddam,	K'brewster.
6 50	P.M.	J. Bruce,	Aberdeen,	Fraserburgh
...	1 25	Do.	Fraserburgh	K'brewster.
P.M.				
12 40	...	J. Gauld,	Aberdeen,	Maud.
3 25	...	Do.	Maud,	Fraserburgh
...	7 0	e Do.	Fraserburgh	Aberdeen.
A.M.	A.M.			
...	7 15	d J.Findlayson,	Peterhead,	Aberdeen.
11 20	...	Do.	K'brewster,	Peterhead.
P.M.	P.M.			
...	7 5	Peterhead Porter, 2nd,	Peterhead,	Maud.
7 0	...	Do.	Maud,	Peterhead.

* 2nd, Aberdeen to Maud. + 2nd, Maud to Aberdeen.

Guards of 4·55 a.m., 5·15 a.m., and 7·53 a.m. (Bucksburn) change weekly.

Guards of 5·40 a.m. and 2·25 p.m.— see Main Line for change of runs.

Guards of 6·50 a.m., 12·40 p.m., 9·35 a.m., and 8·10 a.m. change weekly.

Brakesman of 6·50 a.m. and 12·40 p.m. change weekly.

Guards of 7·5 a.m., 7·25 a.m., and 12·55 p.m. change weekly.

c To come on duty at 4·45 a.m., and to be relieved of duty on arrival at Kittybrewster of 2·30 p.m. ex Inveramsay. d Alone between Peterhead and Maud.

f On Mondays to come on duty at 2·30 a.m., and be relieved from 4·0 a.m. till 5·30 a.m.; also to be relieved of duty on arrival at Kittybrewster of 9·55 a.m. ex Boddam.

g Alone, Longside to Maud. h Mons. only.

§ On Wednesdays, Guard and Brakesman of 5·15 a.m. Down Goods Train will not go beyond Longside, and Peterhead Porter will work 7·30 a.m. Up and 5·15 a.m. Down Trains between Peterhead and Longside.

Main Line—*continued.*

BIRCHFIELD PLATFORM (between Rothes and Longmorn). The Trains (8·5 a.m. and 2·30 p.m. from Aberdeen and 9·35 a.m. and 2·20 p.m. from Elgin excepted) will stop at Birchfield when there are Passengers on the Platform to be taken up, or in the Trains to be set down. Passengers to be taken up must be on the Platform at least Ten Minutes before the Train passes; and Passengers to be set down must inform the Guard that such is the case before entering the Train, otherwise the Train will not be stopped.

Buchan Section.

Mls	STATIONS.	1	2	3	4	5	6	7	8	9
			a.m.		a.m.		p.m.			p.m
	Elgin v. B'kie	....	....	.....	9 28	.....	.....	.....	....	2 25
	,, v. Craig.	....	....	.....	9 35	.....	.....	.....	....	2 20
	Keith Town	....	....	.....	10 37	.....	.....	.....	....	3 27
	Keith	....	6 20	.....	10 47	.....	1 3	.....	....	....
	Buckie	....	....	.....	9 58	.....	.....	.....	....	2 53
	Huntly	....	6 44	.....	11 20	.....	1 28	.....	....	4 0
	Macduff	....	6 15	.....	8 40	.....	12 30	.....	....	4 20
	Oldmeldrum	....	7 20	.....	8 50	.....	1 30	.....	....	5 50
	Alford	....	7 0	.....	8.48	.....	1 45	.....	....	5 30
		a.m.	a.m.		p.m.		p.m.			p.m.
...	Aberdeen de.	6 50	8 25	.....	12 43	.....	4 25	.....	....	7 0
1¼	Kittybrewster	6 55	....	.....	12 49	.....	4 31	.....	....	7 6
2½	Woodside	6 59	....	.....	.....	.....	.....	.....	....	7 10
4¼	Bucksburn	7 3	....	.....	.....	.....	.....	.....	....	7 14
6¼	Dyce Jun. ar.	7 8	8 36	....	12 59	.....	4 41	.....	....	7 19
...	Dyce Jun. de.	7 9	8 37	.....	1 0	.....	4 42	.....	....	7 20
7¼	Parkhill	7 12	....	.....	1 3	.....	4 45	.....	....	7 23
11½	Newmachar	7 22	A	.....	1 14	.....	4 57	.....	....	7 34
14½	Udny	7 29	....	.....	1 22	.....	5 5	.....	....	7 41
16¼	Logierieve	7 33	....	.....	1 26	.....	5 9	.....	....	7 45
17¾	Esslemont	7 37	....	.....	1 30	.....	5 13	.....	....	7 49
19⅝	Ellon	7 42	9 2	.....	1 36	.....	5 19	.....	....	7 54
23	Arnage	7 51	B	.....	1 45	.....	5 28	.....	....	8 6
27	Auchnagatt	8 2	9 18	.....	1 56	.....	5 39	.....	....	8 17
31¼	Maud Jun. ar.	8 10	9 25	.....	2 4	.....	5 47	.....	....	8 25
...	Maud Jun. de.	8 15	9 30	.....	2 9	.....	5 53	.....	....	8 30
33	Brucklay	8 20	....	.....	2 14	.....	5 58	.....	....	8 35
37	Strichen	8 28	9 44	.....	2 22	.....	6 6	.....	....	8 43
39⅝	Mormond	8 34	....	.....	2 28	.....	6 12	.....	....	....
42	Lonmay	8 40	9 55	.....	2 34	.....	6 18	.....	....	8 52
44¼	Rathen	8 47	....	.....	2 41	.....	6 24	.....	....	8 59
47¼	Fraserbro' ar.	8 56	10 5	.....	2 50	.....	6 33	.....	....	9 8
...	Maud Jun. de.	8 15	9 30	.....	2 9	.....	5 53	.....	....	8 30
35¼	Mintlaw	8 23	9 37	.....	2 17	.....	6 0	.....	....	8 37
38½	Longside	8 30	9 44	.....	2 24	.....	6 7	.....	....	8 44
40¼	Newseat	8 35	....	.....	2 29	.....	6 12	.....	....	....
42¼	Inverugie	8 41	9 53	.....	2 35	.....	6 18	.....	....	8 53
44¼	Peterhead ar.	8 46	9 58	.....	2 40	.....	6 23	.....	....	8 58

STATIONS.	1	2	3	4	5	6	7	8
			C		D			
	a.m.		a.m.	p.m.	p.m.		p.m.	
Peterhead de.	7 10	....	9 30	12 45	3 35	....	7 0	....
Inverugie	7 15	....	9 35	12 50	3 40	....	7 8	....
Newseat	7 19	....	.....	12 54	3 44	....	7 13	....
Longside	7 25	....	9 44	1 0	3 49	....	7 20	....
Mintlaw	7 34	....	9 53	1 9	3 57	....	7 32	....
Maud Jun. ar.	7 42	....	10 0	1 17	4 4	....	7 43	....
Fraserbro' de.	6 58	....	9 20	12 33	3 30	....	6 58	....
Rathen	7 6	....	9 27	12 41	3 36	....	7 6	....
Lonmay	7 12	....	9 33	12 47	3 42	....	7 12	....
Mormond	7 20	....	E	12 55	....	....	7 20	....
Strichen	7 26	....	9 44	1 1	3 53	....	7 26	....
Brucklay	7 37	....	9 55	1 12	....	....	7 37	....
Maud Jun. ar	7 42	....	10 0	1 17	4 4	....	7 42	....
Maud Jun. de.	7 50	....	10 7	1 25	4 10	....	7 49	....
Auchnagatt	8 0	....	10 16	1 35	4 19	....	7 58	....
Arnage	8 7	....	10 23	1 45	....	....	8 6	....
Ellon	8 17	....	10 32	1 55	4 32	....	8 15	....
Esslemont	8 22	....	.....	2 1	....	....	8 20	....
Logierieve	8 27	....	.....	2 6	4 39	....	8 25	....
Udny	8 34	....	10 43	2 13	4 45	....	8 32	....
Newmachar	8 48	....	10 53	2 24	4 57	....	8 42	....
Parkhill	8 56	....	.....	2 32	....	....	8 50	....
Dyce Jun. ar.	8 59	....	11 1	2 35	5 5	....	8 53	....
Dyce Jun. de.	9 0	....	11 2	2 36	5 6	...	8 54	....
Bucksburn	9 5	....	.....	.....	....	....	.....	....
Woodside	9 9	....	.....	.....	....	....	.....	....
Kittybrewster	9 18	....	11 10	2 45	....	....	9 3	....
Aberdeen ar.	9 20	....	11 17	2 52	5 20	....	9 10	....
Alford ar.	11 10		.....	5 2	7 13	....	.....	....
Oldmeldrum	11 0		2 10p	5 10	7 0	....	.....	....
Macduff	12 15		3 35	6 20	8 5	....	.....	....
Huntly	11 23		3 36	5 6	7 37	....	.....	....
Buckie	12 53		....	6 31	8 53	....	.....	....
Keith	11 55		.....	5 35	8 22	....	.....	....
Keith Town	12 8		3 58	5 43	....	....	.....	....
Elgin v. Craig	1 10		4 52	6 55	....	....	.....	....
,, v. B'kie	1 30		.....	7 10	9 22	....	.....	....

A On Mondays and Wednesdays calls at Newmachar with and for Passengers.
B On Wednesdays calls at Arnage with and for Passengers.
C Passengers from Buchan Section for Insch and beyond travel to Aberdeen to join 2·30 p.m. Train.
D Passengers from Buchan Section for beyond Huntly travel to Aberdeen to join 6·45 p.m. Train.
E On Wednesdays calls at Mormond with and for Passengers.

PETERHEAD AND FRASERBURGH TRAINS.

Miles.	STATIONS.							
		a.m.			p.m.		p.m.	p.m.
.....	Peterhead de.	7 10	.....	.....	12 45	.....	3 35	7 0
2	Inverugie	7 15	.....	.....	12 50	.....	3 40	7 8
3¼	Newseat	7 19	.....	.....	12 54	.....	3 44	7 13
5¾	Longside	7 25	.....	.....	1 0	.....	3 49	7 20
9	Mintlaw	7 34	.....	.....	1 9	.....	3 57	7 32
13	Maud Jun. ar.	7 42	.....	.....	1 17	.....	4 4	7 43
.....	Maud Jun. de.	8 15	.....	.....	2 9	.....	5 53	8 30
14¾	Brucklay	8 20	.....	.....	2 14	.....	5 58	8 35
18¾	Strichen	8 28	.....	.....	2 22	.....	6 6	8 43
21¼	Mormond	8 34	.....	.....	2 28	.....	6 12	.....
23¾	Lonmay	8 40	.....	.....	2 34	.....	6 18	8 52
26¼	Rathen	8 47	.....	.....	2 41	.....	6 24	8 59
29	Fraserbro' ar.	8 56	.....	.....	2 50	.....	6 33	9 8

FRASERBURGH AND PETERHEAD TRAINS.

Mls	STATIONS.							
		a.m.	.....	p.m.		p.m.	p.m.	
...	Fraserburgh de.	6 58	.....	12 33	.....	3 30	6 58	.....
2¾	Rathen	7 6	.....	12 41	.....	3 36	7 6	.....
5½	Lonmay	7 12	.....	12 47	.....	3 42	7 12	.....
7¾	Mormond	7 20	.....	12 55	.....	.....	7 20	.....
10½	Strichen	7 26	.....	1 1	.....	3 53	7 26	.....
14½	Brucklay	7 37	.....	1 12	.....	.....	7 37	.....
16	Maud Jun. ar.	7 42	.....	1 17	.....	4 4	7 42	.....
...	Maud Jun. de.	8 15	.....	2 9	.....	5 53	8 30	.....
20	Mintlaw	8 23	.....	2 17	.....	6 0	8 37	.....
23½	Longside	8 30	.....	2 24	.....	6 7	8 44	.....
25½	Newseat	8 35	.....	2 29	.....	6 12	.....	.....
27	Inverugie	8 41	.....	2 35	.....	6 18	8 53	.....
29	Peterhead arrive	8 46	.....	2 40	.....	6 23	8 58	.....

ST. COMBS LIGHT RAILWAY.

Mls.	STATIONS.											Sats. only.	
			a.m.	a.m.		a.m.	p.m.		p.m.		p.m.		¶	
....	Fraserburgh, depart	....	6 0	7 55	....	10 30	1 0	....	4 15	....	6 50	....	9 30p	....
3⅝	Cairnbulg ,,	....	6 14	8 9	....	10 47	1 14	....	4 32	....	7 4	....	9 41	....
5⅛	St. Combs, arrive	....	6 20	8 15	....	10 53	1 20	....	4 38	....	7 10	....	9 50	....

One Class only.

Mls.	STATIONS.											Sats. only.	
			a.m.	a.m.		a.m.	p.m.		p.m.		p.m.		¶	
....	St. Combs, depart	....	6 28	8 25	....	11 15	1 40	....	4 50	....	7 20	....	10 0p	....
1½	Cairnbulg, ,,	....	6 35	8 32	....	11 27	1 47	....	5 2	....	7 27	....	10 7	....
5⅛	Fraserburgh, arrive	....	6 48	8 45	....	11 40	2 0	....	5 15	....	7 40	....	10 20	....

¶ Commences to run on 2nd December.

One Class only.

KIRKTON BRIDGE and PHILORTH BRIDGE PLATFORMS.—Trains will stop at these Platforms when a request is made to the Guard, or when there are Passengers upon them. Passengers joining the Trains at these Platforms will pay their fare at Cairnbulg or Fraserburgh as the case may be.

Table 37 ABERDEEN, FRASERBURGH and PETERHEAD

Week Days only

Miles		am D	am	am	pm E	pm S	pm	pm	pm	pm
—	**Aberdeen** dep	6 55	8 25		1223	1223		4 4		6 10
1¼	Kittybrewster	7 0	8 30		1228	1228		4 9		6 15
6¼	Dyce	7 8	8 38		1236	1236		4 17		6 23
11½	Newmachar	7 18	8 48		1246	1246		4 27		
14½	Udny		8 54		1252	1252		4 33		6 38
16¼	Logierieve	7 27	8 58		1256	1256		4 37		6 42
19¼	Ellon	7 35	9 4		1 2	1 2		4 43		6 48
23	Arnage	7 43	zz		zz	zz		4 51		6 56
26¾	Auchnagatt	7 50	9 17		1 17	1 17		4 58		7 3
31	Maud Junction arr	7 57	9 28		1 24	1 24		5 5		7 10
	Maud Junction dep	7 59	9 29	9 34	1 26	1 26	1 30	5 6	5 10	7 16
32¾	Brucklay	8 3	9 33			1 30		5 10		7 20
36¾	Strichen	8 10	9 40		1 36	1 37		5 17		7 27
39¼	Mormond Halt					hh		hh		
41¾	Lonmay	8 18	9 48		1 44	1 46		5 25		7 35
44	Rathen	8 23			1 49	1 51		5 30		
45½	Philorth Halt	zz			zz	zz		zz		zz
47	**Fraserburgh** arr	8 30	9 58		1 56	1 58		5 37		7 45
35	Mintlaw dep			9 40					5 16	
38¼	Longside			9 46			1 40		5 22	
40¾	Newseat Halt			9C51			1 45		zz	
42	Inverugie			9 54			1 48		5 29	
44¼	**Peterhead** arr			9 58			1 52		5 33	

Week Days only

Miles	Miles		am	am	am	am	pm	pm D	pm	pm	pm S	pm E
—	—	**Peterhead** dep	6 40		1010		1245		3 15			
1¾	—	Inverugie	6 44		1014		1249		3 19			
3½	—	Newseat Halt	6 48						3 23			
6	—	Longside	6 52		1021				3 27			
9¼	—	Mintlaw	6 58		1027		1 0		3 33			
—	—	**Fraserburgh** dep		6 40		10 5		1235		3 8	6 35	6 40
—	1¼	Philorth Halt		zz				zz		zz	zz	
—	3	Rathen				1012		1242		3 15	6 42	
—	5¼	Lonmay		6 49		1017				3 20	6 47	
—	7¾	Mormond Halt						hh				
—	10¼	Strichen		6 58		1026		1255		3 29	6 56	6 56
—	14¼	Brucklay		7 6		1034		1 3		3 37	7 4	7 4
13¾	16	Maud Junction arr	7 5	7 10	1034	1038	1 7	1 7	3 40	3 42	7 9	7 9
		Maud Junction dep		7 14		1040		1 9		3 47	7 13	7 13
17½	—	Auchnagatt		7 21		1047		1 18		3 54	7 20	7 20
21¼	—	Arnage		7 27		zz		1 24		zz	7 26	7 26
25	—	Ellon		7 34		11 0		1 31		4 7	7 33	7 33
28	—	Logierieve		7 40				1 37		4 13	7 39	7 39
29¼	—	Udny		7 45				1 42		4 18		
32¾	—	Newmachar		7 52				1K48		4 30		
38	—	Dyce		8 0		1123		1 56		4 38		
43	—	Kittybrewster		8 7		1130		2 3		4 45	8 2	8 2
44¼	—	**Aberdeen** arr		8 11		1134		2 7		4 49	8 6	8 6

C Calls on Wednesdays and Saturdays only
D Diesel Service
E Except Saturdays

hh Calls on Saturdays only when required
K Calls on Wednesdays and Saturdays only to set down on request to Guard

S or S Saturdays only
zz Stops to set down on request to Guard, or when there are passengers to take up

For OTHER TRAINS between Aberdeen and Dyce, see Table 36

Table 38 FRASERBURGH and ST. COMBS

DIESEL SERVICE—SECOND CLASS ONLY

Week Days only

Miles		am	am	am	am	pm S	pm E	pm S	pm	pm	pm	pm	pm	pm
—	**Fraserburgh** dep	6 25	8 0	8 50	1030	1210	1 0	1 5	2 15	4 15	5 15	6 15	8 25	9 20
1	Kirkton Bridge Halt	nn	nn	nn	nn	nn	nn	nn	nn	nn	nn	nn	nn	nn
2¼	Philorth Bridge Halt	nn	nn	nn	nn	nn	nn	nn	nn	nn	nn	nn	nn	nn
3½	Cairnbulg	6 39	8 14	9 4	1044	1224	1 14	1 19	2 29	4 29	5 29	6 29	8 39	9 34
5	**St. Combs** arr	6 45	8 20	9 10	1050	1230	1 20	1 25	2 35	4 35	5 35	6 35	8 45	9 40

Week Days only

Miles		am	am	am	am	pm S	pm E	pm S	pm	pm	pm	pm	pm	pm
—	**St. Combs** dep	6 55	8 25	9 15	1115	1235	1 40	1 45	2 40	4 40	5 45	6 45	8 55	9 45
1½	Cairnbulg	7 2	8 32	9 22	1122	1242	1 47	1 52	2 47	4 47	5 52	6 52	9 2	9 52
2¾	Philorth Bridge Halt	nn	nn	nn	nn	nn	nn	nn	nn	nn	nn	nn	nn	nn
4	Kirkton Bridge Halt	nn	nn	nn	nn	nn	nn	nn	nn	nn	nn	nn	nn	nn
5	**Fraserburgh** arr	7 15	8 45	9 35	1135	1255	2 0	2 5	3 0	5 0	6 5	7 5	9 15	10 5

E Except Saturdays

nn Stops to set down on request to Guard, or when there are passengers to take up

S Saturdays only

IMPORTANT NOTICE

Issue of Tickets

On and from Monday, 7th November, 1960, the issue of all types of tickets will be discontinued at the undernoted stations:—

ST. COMBS	MINTLAW
CAIRNBULG	MAUD JUNCTION
RATHEN	AUCHNAGATT
LONMAY	ARNAGE
STRICHEN	ELLON
BRUCKLAY	LOGIERIEVE
INVERUGIE	UDNY
LONGSIDE	NEWMACHAR

As from the date mentioned, tickets will be issued on the train by the guard.

Season tickets for journeys from any of the stations referred to should be ordered in advance of the first day of travel from the Station Masters, Aberdeen, Peterhead or Fraserburgh.

Published by British Railways (Scottish Region). B.R. 35009—B30253—Y—October. 1960.   Printed in Great Britain by The Herald Press. Arbroath.

SNOW

Monday, 18th January 1960 was not an unusually wintry day for the north-east of Scotland. True, there had been some heavy falls of snow and some of the roads had become blocked, while north of Inverness there was drifting that held up traffic here and there, but things were no worse than was expected in January at that time. On the Tuesday morning it started to snow again and on the vulnerable Buchan lines two diesel and two fish trains were now halted. By the afternoon it seemed as if the storm had passed and that frost was setting in, but in the evening the wind rose to gale force, bring telegraph poles down like skittles and tangling power and telephone lines. On Wednesday, 20th January glorious sunshine and windless blue skies set of a scene to rival many of the continental winter sport resorts. There was only one snag — almost no transport.

The Buchan lines, usually the worst hit, had again taken a beating. On Tuesday, the four coach diesel train consisting of the 9.17 a.m. two coach unit from Fraserburgh and the 9.30 a.m. two coach unit from Peterhead, ran into a deep drift in the cutting 300 yards north of Newmachar Station at about 11.00 a.m. Newmachar is 5¼ miles north of Dyce which is 6¼ miles from Aberdeen. It was reported by the station-master that the train had thirty-five passengers aboard, but the actual number proved to be 57, and that the drift was 8 ft. high in front of the train. It was impossible to evacuate the passengers because of the blizzard. The storm abated about 1.30 p.m. but, as it was impossible to reach Newmachar by road because it was blocked beyond Dyce, a relief train was arranged and it left Aberdeen at 3.30 p.m. On board was Mr Graham, the Assistant District Engineer and Chief Permanent Way Inspector Ogilvie with about 25 men. A number of telegraph poles were fouling the line between Aberdeen and Dyce and the blizzard was as severe as before. Consequently the relief train was delayed en route and several halts had to be made to cut away telegraph wires wrapped around the engine. This train arrived at Dyce about 7.30 p.m. but as it was hauled by a Type 2 diesel, it was necessary to wait for a large snow plough before the train could enter the Dyce/Newmachar section which was known to be heavily drifted and obstructed by poles. During this interval the men were given hot soup, etc., which was sent by Landrover from Aberdeen. A supply of tea and food was also put on the train for the stranded passengers.

It was decided to send the snow plough ahead of the relief train and this left Dyce at 8.35 p.m. and was followed by the relief train at 8.50 p.m. Progress was very slow because of obstructions and as there was no telephone communication between Newmachar and the Aberdeen Control and nothing had been heard of the train up to midnight, we were rather apprehensive about what might have happened. The District Traffic Superintendent's chief clerk went out in the District Engineer's land rover to try to make contact by road but he had to turn back as the road was completely blocked by drifts and stranded vehicles. A further attempt was then made by sending another

On 19th January 1960, a d.m.u. was caught in a snowdrift at Newmachar. Fifty-seven passengers were stranded in the train until late the following day. The train comprised two twin sets of units, one each from Peterhead and Fraserburgh respectively.

Courtesy Aberdeen Journals

engine into the section at 1.00 a.m. and this engine went through to Newmachar and returned at 3.45 a.m. to report that ploughing was being done south of Newmachar, in heavy drifts, in an effort to get the relief train nearer the stranded train. It was only possible to get this train within about a quarter of a mile of the passenger train, that is about 40 yards south of the platform and most of the station had drifts from 4 to 10 ft. high. The blizzard still continued and it was impossible for the men to make any progress in casting, as they were wet through and tired, having been out since early morning. Mr Graham and some of the men set out with food and tea for the stranded train which they reached in almost half an hour and had to gain access through the driver's window as the drift prevented the door from being opened. They found the passengers quite comfortable as the heating and lights were working and one of the passengers, a nurse, had some tins of soup with her which the guard had been able to heat up on his electric grill. However, rations had only been provided for 35 passengers which was the number reported by the guard, and it was found that there were 57 on the train. Therefore Mr Graham called for volunteers to make the difficult journey to Newmachar village, about half a mile from the station, to obtain further supplies which were readily obtained from the trades people, in spite of the late hour.

The next operation was to persuade the passengers to leave the train and join the single coach and brake van on the relief train, a quarter of a mile away over the drift. However, when it was explained that it might take half a day or more before the train could be pulled clear, all passengers agreed to make the somewhat hazardous journey and, assisted by the men, all were safely transferred and crowded into the single coach and brake van along with the gang. One man, who was lame, was carried piggy-back by squad lorry driver Lamb. Fortunately, there were clear spells during lulls in the storm while the evacuation was taking place. The relief train was propelled back and arrived in Aberdeen about 6.00 a.m. on Wednesday, 20th January and none of the passengers, most of whom had come from Fraserburgh and Peterhead and had been on the train for twenty hours, appeared to show any signs of distress. In fact, they expressed their appreciation of the efforts which had been made to assist them.

In view of the indefinite time which the relief operation would take, and the fact that the staff engaged would require relieving, contact had previously been made by the Assistant District Traffic Superintendent, Mr Turner, with the RNAS station at Lossiemouth and with the RAF Mountain Rescue Unit at Kinloss with a view to obtaining assistance of helicopters, either to drop food, or to take off the passengers. However, these units could only operate in daylight and could not undertake night operations in the weather then prevailing. As it was essential to free the train as early as possible in order to gain access to the snow blocks further north, and as men could not be obtained in sufficient numbers in Aberdeen until the next morning, the Assistant DTS, Mr Turner, asked for the assistance of the military at Gordon Barracks and the Commanding Officer arranged to alert 50 men to be available when called upon. These men were conveyed by their own transport to Kittybrewster at 5.00a.m. and left for the site about an hour later when the engines and crews had been changed. The soldiers were commanded by their own officer, but Mr Graham offered to return with the detachment and Inspector Finnie was called out to assist. Good progress was made as the storm had abated and there was less drifting. Snow casting and ploughing were continued and the troops returned to barracks about midday.

It was possible to plough most of the station after handcasting had reduced the drift but care had to be exercised in approaching the diesel train just ahead. A squad of men from Montrose, along with the Aberdeen relaying gangs, were sent in after the troops had returned, and the diesel train was reached and pulled out at 5.30p.m. on Wednesday, 20th January. Ploughing with the large plough on a Class 5 engine assisted by a second engine was continued to Ellon, which was reached about 9.15p.m. Three quarters of a mile beyond Ellon a very stubborn drift was encountered, the snow by now having frozen and become very hard packed. It was decided to return as the men, mostly artisan staff, had been out since morning, and Mr Graham was instructed to come in with them as he had been out continuously for about 37 hours. Thereafter clearance operations were continued until the whole line was cleared on Friday afternoon, 22nd January, and by the same evening all passenger lines in the Aberdeen district had been cleared.

On the Tuesday there were detained, at Ellon, two fish trains, but the 8.22a.m. from Aberdeen to Fraserburgh managed to get through, although not in time to relieve the St. Combs branch. On this line, a normal service was operated with somewhat abnormal loads — about 250 passengers on each of the evening rush-hour trains, (twin coach d.m.u.).

Thursday 21st January, was a miserable, wet, drizzly day. The thaw started fairly rapidly and transport began to move again. By Friday, the Peterhead branch was cleared; no passenger trains were run, but some freight and live-stock was moved. The Fraserburgh line was blocked just north of Strichen and it was Saturday evening before the first passenger train could pass over it; this train, the 6.38p.m. from Aberdeen was a d.m.u. including a portion for Peterhead and was late through lack of fuel. Normal services were not resumed until Monday, 26th January.

TICKET STORIES
one of an occasional series
by
A. W. Coutts

The day started quietly enough for A.F.C. as he left the Palace Hotel at ten minutes to eight on a cold but sunny December morning. He arrived at the Joint Station and purchased his ticket to Cruden Bay. The sun shone although the air began to freeze. But all this could not distract A.F.C's. interest from the locomotive which was at the head of his train — the 8.10a.m. from Aberdeen to Fraserburgh and Peterhead. It was one of Pickersgill's new 4-4-0 locomotives, No. 31 and it was obviously not long out of the shops at Inverurie for the paint seemed to glow in the icy air.

By Dyce, the clouds had gathered and snow began to fall. The train continued on its northerly haul as the light faded further and darkness seemed to fall on the land. The snow seemed to attack the train like a plague of locusts intent on destruction. Udny, the first stop, was reached as the snow continued to pile up and the train slowly filled up with the waiting public.

It was not until A.F.C. reached Ellon and saw the train to Cruden Bay that he expressed any doubts about whether or not his destination would be reached, for here he found a seemingly diminutive 0-4-4 tank locomotive, No. 92 and a single coach standing at the other side of the island platform.

Although scheduled to leave Ellon at 8.55a.m., it was almost 9.30a.m. before the train eventually left for Boddam and so, over thirty-five minutes

30   A snowplough engine, with an assisting engine at the rear, in action between Parkhill and Newmachar on 27th January 1942. The relieving pit, cut in the drift, can be seen in the left foreground.

Courtesy Aberdeen Journals

late, the train contrived to pull itself away towards Auchmacoy. By ten o'clock the storm had abated and Pitlurg was reached. A.F.C. had convinced himself that all was well but it was not to be, for soon after Hatton the heavens opened their pearly gates and all hell was let loose. Once again the train continued through a tunnel of white light and on to its destination.

It was with a happy heart and a gladsome mind that A.F.C. finally saw the dim lights of Cruden Bay as the tiny train finally pushed and pulled its way into the station. With a cheery wave to the station staff, the train pulled out on its remaining five mile journey to the fishing port at Boddam, leaving A.F.C. with the task of proceeding to the Cruden Bay Hotel to enquire of the state of upkeep during the winter months.

Although he had bought a 'day excursion' ticket, he decided to stay overnight until the storm had passed. Indeed, this would be one inspection he would never forget.

Cruden Bay Station, with a train ready to leave for Ellon. The first two coaches are through coaches for Aberdeen. The scene is circa 1909–1912.

Sir Malcolm Barclay Harvey

MOTOR CHAR-A-BANC OWNED BY THE
COMPANY.

CRUDEN BAY HOTEL.

PALACE HOTEL.

MOTOR OMNIBUS OWNED BY THE COMPANY.

THE CRUDEN BAY HOTEL AND ITS TRAMWAY
by
M. J. Mitchell

An appeal for information on the Cruden Bay Hotel Tramway was published in the February 1977 *Great North Review* and more recently the journal contained an appeal for information on the GNSR hotels themselves. This short article is intended to gather together the relatively small amount of information on the Cruden Bay Hotel Tramway and to provide some information on the hotel itself. It is hoped thereby to jog the memories of some readers and, perhaps, to encourage further research.

In 1890, the GNSR Board appointed a 'Hotel Committee' to 'arrange as to structural alterations, new furnishings and the conduct of the hotel business generally'. The committee soon had the Palace Hotel, Aberdeen in its charge, and this opened for business on 22nd August 1891 *(See Note 1, Page 40)*, proving to be an immediate success. The GNSR was encouraged to expand further into the hotel business and saw a useful means of generating traffic as well as making money from the hotels themselves. An attempt was made to purchase the Invercauld Arms at Ballater, but this finally fell through in April 1896 *(See Note 2, Page 40)*.

Meanwhile, in January 1895, the Board decided to look into the possibility of building a luxury hotel near Port Erroll on the Buchan coast north of Ellon. By the end of that month, estimates and plans were submitted for the 'Port Erroll Hotel' as the Cruden Bay Hotel was known at first. It was to be a 55-bedroom structure, built of pink Peterhead granite at a cost of £13,816. The plan was generally approved, and the engineer was instructed to provide drawings and specifications. The final estimates, submitted in April 1896, quoted £16,000 for the hotel, plus £650 for lifts, £350 for heating, £4,000 for furnishings and £1,000 for 'ground, walls, etc.,' bringing the total cost to £22,000. It was hoped that the District Council would provide water and sewerage to the remote promontory on which the hotel was to be built but, in the end, the GNSR laid its own services at a cost of £1,200. Lighting was to be by paraffin lamps, but 'if a laundry is erected, electric lighting can be provided at a probable outlay of £1,000 for a dynamo and wiring' with an additional £400 for fittings.

Within the next few months, the contracts for the construction work were let, and a Miss Duffus was appointed manageress in September 1897 at a salary of £100 per annum to take charge of the equipping of the, as yet unbuilt, hotel from 1st January 1898. She resigned, however, in November 1897 and a Miss Catherine Campbell of Brighton was appointed in her place, reigning until the end of January 1900. Provisioning contracts were let for food supplies, wines and spirits, furnishings and equipment. The scale of the task of equipping such a large hotel may be seen from the details of the supply of cutlery by Walker & Hall of Sheffield:

Cruden Bay Hotel photographed from the air.

G.N.S.R.A. Collection

Cruden Bay Hotel photographed from the east, showing a tram standing outside the main entrance.

G.N.S.R.A. Collection

60 dozen table knives	@	6/6d	(32½p)	per dozen
60 dozen tea knives	@	6/1d	(30½p)	per dozen
60 dozen table forks	@	6/-	(30p)	per dozen
60 dozen dessert forks	@	3/10d	(19p)	per dozen
12 dozen table spoons	@	6/-	(30p)	per dozen
120 dozen dessert spoons	@	3/10d	(19p)	per dozen
50 dozen tea spoons	@	2/-	(10p)	per dozen

By the end of February 1898, work was well advanced and plastering of the walls was in progress.

Perhaps conscious of the distance of their new hotel from the station, (over half a mile), and the need to offer the latest in comforts to the top class guest whose custom they were aiming for, the GNSR Finance Committee decided, in August 1898, to send the directors and the Company's engineers to the Isle of Man to inspect the 'Electric and Light Railways' there. The delegation must have been impressed, for on 14th September 1898, the Board 'considered further plans for a laundry, a combined passenger and luggage lift and an electrical tramway between the hotel and the station including an extra engine and dynamo at Cruden Bay'. The cost was put at £9,005.

It was decided to go ahead with the whole scheme, including the tramway 'provided that satisfactory arrangements can be made for the necessary land . . . and for . . . crossing the road'. The latter proved no problem, for the Aberdeen County Council agreed to the road crossing of the Newburgh-Port Erroll road on three conditions:

1 — that the GNSR accepted full accident liability.
2 — that the GNSR paved the road between the rails and for four feet each side, and
3 — that the County Council could revoke their permission at any time.

The hotel opened for guests at the beginning of March 1899 amid much press attention, and the tramway, some three months later, in June.

The tramway was constructed very much as a railway with trams running on it. The track was bullhead rail on chaired sleepers, with open ballasted formation between the road crossing and the station yard. At the hotel and in the station yard, the track was paved to rail level with granite setts. The gauge was a nominal 3 ft. 6½ in. Starting from the station, a short loop with a siding was laid to the west of the station building and the line followed the western edge of the approach road and entered a shallow cutting by the side of the Hatton-Port Erroll road. It then crossed a field, then the Newburgh-Port Erroll road and swung round the front of the hotel to terminate by the front door. A triangular junction just over the road crossing led to a branch to the two-road car shed and laundry. A further siding was later laid between the laundry and the back of the hotel. Access to the car shed and the west side of the laundry was by turntable.

Cruden Bay Hotel trams stand outside the hotel laundry.

W. Hennigan

To link the hotel and station at Cruden Bay, the 'Great North' built and operated a short narrow gauge (3 ft. 6½ in.) electric tramway, a venture unique amongst Scottish railways. Two single deck four-wheel tramcars worked the system along with several goods trailers, electric power being generated at the hotel's boiler house and distributed by overhead wire and trolley collector. The tramcars were built in 1899 at Kittybrewster Works and were unusual in having a section reserved for luggage and laundry baskets, clearly visible in the photograph. In use until 1940, the tram bodies still survive as summer houses in the village of Hatton.

Rolling stock consisted of two single deck four-wheel trams, a four-wheel van, and open four-wheel trailer for coal and possibly, *(See Note 3, Page 40)*, two further bogies for boilers and heavy items. All the rolling stock was built at Kittybrewster with the exception of the tramcar trucks, which were Peckham 'Excelsior' type 7B trucks of 6 ft. 6 in. wheelbase and 2 ft. 6 in. wheel diameter, fitted with 2 x 15 h.p. motors. The tramcar bodies were of a clerestoried 'combination' type, with a longitudinally seated passenger compartment for 16 persons occupying most of the available space, but with a raised platform at one end for luggage and laundry baskets. Extensive use was made of wrought ironwork, and etched and bevelled glass, the passenger doors being particularly ornate. A bulb-type horn was fitted at each end, and the controller was an unusual vertical type possibly constructed by the GNSR itself. The trams were finished in standard coach livery, with full lining out and 'CRUDEN BAY HOTEL' in block shaded letters on the rocker panels *(See Note 5, Page 40)*.

Power supply was from a 33 kW combined vertical Bellis & Morcom engine and Parker generator, distributed by copper wire suspended from tramway-type bracket arms, again heavily decorated with wrought iron.

At the start of the operations the trams must have been stabled in the open, because it was not until the middle of July 1899 that the Finance Committee resolved to provide 'a shed for the electric cars' at a cost of £500.

Fares were not charged for hotel guests, but non-residents paid 3d, plus 3d for luggage. In spite of this, the tramway took surprisingly high receipts. In the *Hotel Journal* for 1899-1900, the following is recorded:

				March 1900	£1	1s	6d
April 1899	£4	3s	6d	April	6	9s	3d
May		15s	6d	May	3	17s	9d
June	3	18s	0d	June	8	13s	9d
July	15	19s	0d	July	9	8s	0d
August		3s	0d	August	16	10s	9d
September	15	1s	6d	September	15	18s	6d
October		1s	0d	October	5	15s	3d
Nov. 1899 – Feb. 1900		Nil		November		9s	9d
(Closed)				December		3s	0d

The very low figure for August 1899 is strange, as is the fact that the line appeared to be earning before it was opened! Perhaps the sums for April and May 1899 refer to a temporary wagonette service.

The hotel results for the first five months of operation were said to be 'most encouraging' and as a result, the tariff was revised for August and September 1899:

	1st floor	2nd floor	3rd floor	4th floor
Full board	15/-	14/-	12/-	10/6
Sitting room	21/-	12/6 to 15/-	9/-	—
Dressing room	3/6	3/6	3/-	—

A sitting room on the first floor cost £6 for a week of seven days. Full board comprized 'Baths and Light, Breakfast, Luncheon, Afternoon Tea and Dinner'. Fires, billiards and bicycle storage or cleaning were extra.

The main attraction of the hotel, apart from the 'healthy climate' and 'bracing air' referred to in the advertisements, were the golf courses, one of 18 holes and a 9 hole 'Ladies' Course', and during the first season Alex. N. Weir of Arbroath was appointed Golf Pro., although he was also green-keeper and club-maker for his annual salary of £70.

The hotel depended for most of its existence on seasonal staff, and during the winter only a skeleton staff remained on the complement to service those hardy guests who paid £2 10s 0d a week for the privilege of experiencing the bracing climate of the Buchan coast in the off-season. In summer, however, the hotel came alive, with accommodation at a premium.

Miss Campbell's successor, Miss Frater, recommended, in February 1901, that 'by utilizing the car shed as a dormitory during July, August and September for the hotel menservants, ten bedrooms in the new wing of the Cruden Bay Hotel would thereby be available for visitors'. The cars were to be outside again. However, Miss Frater did not reign long (probably to the relief of the staff) and she was 'dispensed with' in November 1901. Her job was advertised at an annual salary of £200-250, more than twice what the GNSR paid her. In spite of the substantial salary, and 56 applicants, the GNSR was unable to find a suitable applicant, and one Mr Trenchard of the Claremont Hydro, Rhyl, was finally appointed at an annual salary of £130.

Although profitable in its early years, the Cruden Bay Hotel soon became an embarrassment to its owners, and never achieved the profit levels of the other two GNSR hotels, the 'Palace' and the 'Station' in Aberdeen. The remoteness of the place, its dependence on the weather and on a specialized well-to-do clientele, made its chances of success poor from the start. Some profit and loss figures have survived and these show how much of a failure the hotel was:

	1904	1905	1909	1910	1911	1915	1916	1921	1922
Hotel	2558	2581	- 273	- 122	70	12	628	- 388	- 293
Golf course	216	240	93	40	99	- 90	- 327	- 232	- 103
Laundry	275	275	- 184	- 141	- 131	260	503	- 13	- 13

(*Figures assumed to be in £ sterling*)

When the Boddam line was closed to passengers in 1932, the main reason for the tramway's existence was taken away, and the hotel's isolation was made complete in the days before mass motoring. The LNER provided a limousine service with Aberdeen in 1934, using a Rolls Royce, (LNER number 2A 0004 – YR 4998), and the trams continued to carry laundry baskets and coal until the army requisitioned the hotel in March 1941. Thereupon the tramway was dismantled for scrap, and the hotel itself, failing to find a buyer after the Army vacated it in 1945, was demolished from 1947 until 1952.

Much of the stone was re-used in the building of a house for Charles Alexander, the well-known haulage contractor, at Bush near Montrose. The two trams still exist at Hatton of Cruden as summer houses, although disintegrating fast, while the four-wheel van survived until a few years ago in a garden at Port Erroll.

Notes:

1 – A photograph of the Palace Hotel appeared on the cover of the *Great North Review* dated August 1965 (No. 6). 'Closed for business' in August 1966, (No. 10) page 29, is about the destruction of the Palace Hotel.

2 – The purchase of the Invercauld Arms was placed 'in abeyance' at a meeting of the GNSR Board on 29th April 1896.

3 – In *LNER Magazine* dated June 1941 (Vol. 31 - No. 6), page 157, there is also a photograph of a tram with driver, conductor and porter in GNSR days.

4 – An interesting record of the tramway's working in the period November 1931 to July 1932 has been preserved at the Scottish Record Office, Edinburgh, in the form of a ledger which records when the tramway generator was switched on and why. One day in summer 1932 serves to illustrate the unique nature of the working of the tramway near the end of its passenger life:

25th June 1932 Saturday
9.20–9.45 a.m. (Passengers), 11.30–11.50 a.m. (Laundry),
2.30–2.55 p.m. (Passengers), 2.55–3.15 p.m. (Laundry),
3.50–4.15 p.m. (Passengers) and 8.10–8.35 p.m. (Passengers)

5 – In LNER days the cars were numbered 1 and 2, and repainted in the standard teak livery.

Bibliography   Minute books and ledgers, GNSR & LNER, SRO, Edinburgh.
Railway Magazine, December 1932, page 462 includes a photograph of Car No. 1 midway between hotel and station.
Railway Magazine, June 1941, page 283, and July 1932 page 413 bear a remarkable resemblance to *LNER Magazine*, June 1941, page 157.
Little and Good published by SLS in 1972
'Rose among the Heather' – article in *Scots Magazine*.
Great North of Scotland Railway H. A. Vallance

Track Plan of Cruden Bay and the Electric Tramway to the Hotel

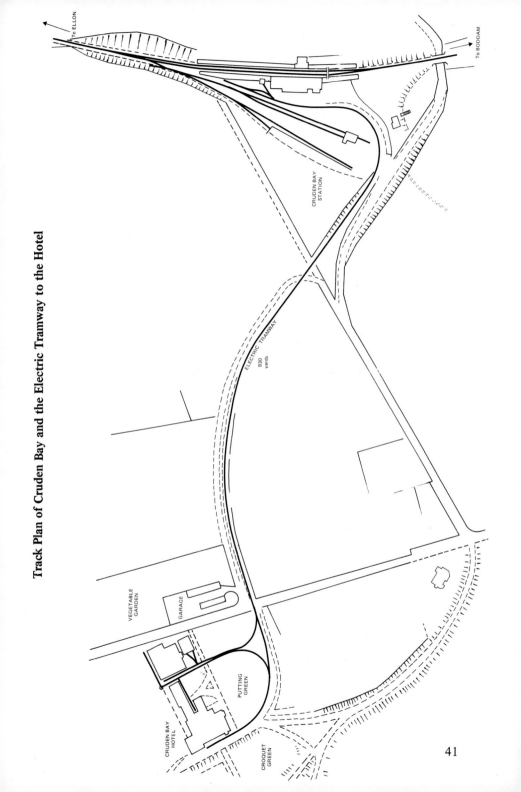

To ELLON

To BODDAM

CRUDEN BAY
STATION

ELECTRIC TRAMWAY

930
yards

VEGETABLE
GARDEN

GARAGE

PUTTING
GREEN

CRUDEN BAY
HOTEL

CROQUET
GREEN

41

CRUDEN BAY
A Postscript by Lord Aberdeen

In the war, Cruden Bay Hotel was taken over by the Depot the Gordon Highlanders in August 1940. The method of training was for Nos. 1 and 2 recruit training companies to alternate between Aberdeen and the hotel. Recruits joined and for a month were docketed, medically jabbed and classified and then sent to the hotel where field training was carried out for the second month.

I commanded No. 2 Coy. from August 1940 to May 1941 and I vividly remember that we were shifted by train from Cruden Bay to Aberdeen on at least one occasion. I would have said in the spring of 1941. Two engines and a rake of ten main line bow-ended corridor stock was provided. The engines arrived tender first and it took a long time to run round the short crossing loop at Cruden Bay. My 400 troops and I had a non-stop and very comfortable run to Aberdeen. I imagine that the idea was to save transport, petrol and, I think, that either Corporation buses or Army transport was provided later.

In the winter of 1940, I took a lease of Springhill House, whence I used to cycle to Bucksburn to catch the 6.50 a.m. to Ellon. I used to get into the brake van of the daily Boddam goods and get put out at Cruden Bay in time for the first parade. I had to be taken to Ellon to catch the last train back to Bucksburn.

It all seems remote now, but one of my jobs at Cruden Bay was to keep the line clear of snow, which fell in great quantities that winter. There was definitely a loop, and shunting was carried out with a wire cable, as at Logierieve. Also, the electric tram was working, as the laundry at Cruden Bay was still working. The hampers were conveyed by the daily goods.

Cruden Bay, before the end.

G.N.S.R.A. Collection

Boddam Station at the end of the line.

G.N.S.R.A. Collection

WHAT DID HAPPEN ON MONDAY, 31ST OCTOBER 1932?

In the November 1971 issue of the *Review*, we published some notes about the closure of the Boddam line to passenger services. The station-master of Boddam at that time, Mr Paul Stuart, has died, but he did state emphatically that the last train ran on a Saturday. On the other hand, the statement that the closure was for the winter months comes as a surprise to quite a number of persons who were employed on the Railway at that time.

The following notes supplied by Mr D. A. Bruce relate to the buses 'Substitute service' which were put on at that time. It was necessary to apply for a licence and the applications were published in a document called 'Notices and Proceedings' (N&P for short).

In N&P No. 92 dated 15th May 1933, applications were made by the LNER, 23 Waterloo Place, Edinburgh, for two services:

TLR743/2 Express carriages between Aberdeen Joint Passenger Railway Station and Cruden Bay Hotel via Aberdeen, Murcar, Balmedie by A 92 and Foveran, Newburgh and Cruden Bay Hotel by A 975, the service to run daily except Sundays from 19th June until 30th September 1933 inclusive:

Aberdeen J. P. Rly. Stn.	Depart	7.50 a.m.	2.10 p.m.
Cruden Bay Hotel	Arrive	8.45 a.m.	3.10 p.m.
	Depart	11.30 a.m.	6.15 p.m.
Aberdeen J. P. Rly. Stn.	Arrive	12.30 p.m.	7.15 p.m.

Passengers would be taken up and set down at the J. P. Rly. Station and the Cruden Bay Hotel. Fares: 3/6d single and 5/- return.

TLR743/3 Express carriages between Ellon Railway Station and Cruden Bay Hotel on the following route from Ellon to Toll of Birness by A 92 thence to Hatton by A 949 thence to Cruden Bay Hotel by unclassified roads via Cruden Church. The service to run on the same dates as above and to take up and set down passengers at Ellon Railway Station and Cruden Bay Hotel. The timetable and fares for this service are not given.

The applications were granted on 31st May 1933 (N&P, No. 96). An application was made to extend the service until 31st October 1933 and this was granted on 30th September (No. 104). In 1934 the application was from 1st June until 6th October but was modified to start on 15th June. In 1935 the application was granted to run from 15th May until 6th October. From 1936 until 1939 the application to continue the service without modification was granted each year. The services ceased on 3rd September 1939 as with other non-essential services.

This would indicate that in 1933 there was a possibility that the rail service might have run in the summer.

CRUDEN BAY HOTEL TRAMWAY

In the June 1941 issue of the *LNER Magazine* there is the following note on the tramway:

'In June 1899, the former G. N. of S. Railway Company put into operation an electric tramway service for passengers and luggage between Cruden Bay Station and the hotel of that name, a distance of rather less than a mile. The track comprised bull-headed rails built to a gauge of 3 ft. 6½ in. Electric power was generated at a plant nearby and distributed by an overhead wire. The rolling stock, built at Kittybrewster Works, consisted of two passenger cars each seating 16 passengers and having a driver's platform at either end. There was also an open trailer car for the carrying of coal and two bogie cars for conveying boilers and other heavy articles. Since 1932, when a direct service by road was introduced by the Company, the tramway has ceased to carry passengers and until recently, has been used solely for the transport of laundry and other goods to and from the hotel. This latter work, however, is now being undertaken by a road vehicle and the works, which once comprised what was possibly the smallest public tramway in Scotland (after 42 years of useful service), are being recovered as scrap which will contribute towards the national effort'.

Random Thoughts on 'The Buchan'
by
J. L. McAllan

Of all the Great North routes, none had more character than the Buchan line (or more accurately, the 'Formartine and Buchan', as it was originally called), to Peterhead and Fraserburgh. Never distinguished for high throughout average speeds, the gradients into and out of one river valley after another saw to that, and yet, it managed to service its territory tolerably well for many decades, and, at times, a high density of traffic, freight and passenger, was worked over it in difficult operating conditions. Generations of travellers felt for it, everything from fury to affection.

My first contact with the route was as a child in the 1920s in early LNER days, when, three or four times a year, we went 'en famille' on holiday to the ancestral home in Fraserburgh. We lived on another part of the system and so the Buchan had no more than a good second place in my Great North affections, but I do remember well those journeys into what seemed a strange land. A common practice was to leave our home station at 5.49 on a Friday evening, alight at Dyce, and after tea in a friendly cafe in Station Road, join the 7 p.m. ex-Aberdeen for Fraserburgh. Thereon, I first met the phenomenon of the Buchan farmer, in great numbers on the way home from the Aberdeen market. I listened in awe to the rich flow of Doric from lips as well lubricated as the wheels below them.

We usually returned on either the 12.35 or the 3.30 ex-Fraserburgh. The 3.30 was reckoned almost an express. It reached the city at 5.20, having omitted several of the smaller stations. To save waiting at Dyce, we often sat on into Aberdeen to catch the 5.45 out again and on such occasions were usually subjected to an excess fare impost at the Schoolhill ticket check. The 12.35, on the other hand, was the very epitome of all that was slow in Buchan. Calling at all stations, it laboured on up hill and down dale, until at last, after Newmachar, as if eager to escape from its own territory, it tore down to Parkhill and then spiritedly along the main line to reach the 'Joint' at 2.45. Once as it toiled up the bank to Logierieve, a sonsy quine opposite was heard to say, 'If the next station's nae Aiberdeen, A'll scream'.

The run down from Newmachar brings to mind the one-time double-track, (unique, I think, in Buchan), between Elrick signal box and Parkhill. This was not doubt put in to facilitate working of important traffic such as fish trains. The first time I noticed this double section, I assumed, with the optimism of youth, that this was the start of a general doubling of the line, and I speculated on how far north it would extend. Little did I realize that in a few years time, such a process was to go into reverse, with the second track lifted and the Elrick and Parkhill boxes closed!

As had been hinted already, the Buchan passenger timetable was never noted for its high speed, and it is doubtful if it ever could have been compared favourably with that of many other similar lines. There is, moreover, one

Dyce Station, the junction for the Formartine & Buchan and Cruden Bay Railways.

G.N.S.R.A. Collection

feature in respect of which it differed from the other main routes out of Aberdeen. It never seems to have catered adequately for what would now be called commuters to and from work in Aberdeen, while for residents on Deeside, the main line and the Alford and Macduff branches could reach Aberdeen between 8 and 9 a.m., and leave again between 5.30 and 6 p.m. The normal pattern of Buchan services did not allow for a morning arrival in Aberdeen until about 9.20, and there were no departures back from the city between 4.25 (4.38 pre-1914) and 7 p.m. In the late 1920s, the LNER altered the 4.25 to 5 p.m. and ran it express to Ellon, with a short-lived steam railcar providing a stopping service at 4.25 as far as Ellon, but even this improvement would scarcely have measured up to a satisfactory commuter service. Only in the last years of BR passenger operation was the evening departure (at 1810) made reasonably suitable for returning office or shop-workers. If I am correct in these observations, it seems strange that the Great North did not provide, in bus-less and car-less times, the commuting facilities for Newmachar, Udny and Ellon which they apparently happily made available to such places as Banchory, Alford and Inverurie.

As with timetables, passenger rolling stock on the Buchan was not of the first order, and was often mixed. A typical formation in the 1920s for each of the Peterhead and Fraserburgh portions (joined or detached at Maud) was a bogie non-corridor third class, a six-wheel corridor composite and a brake

GNSR locomotives Nos. 99 and 68 stand outside Fraserburgh shed and have been specially decorated for the Coronation of King Edward VII and Queen Alexandra in 1902.

G.N.S.R.A. Collection

Sir David Stewart, originally GNSR Class 'F' No. 47, stands outside Peterhead shed in 1950.

N. R. Knight

van. So you took your choice between a reasonably smooth run, toilet-less and a rather rougher trip with facilities.

For many years after the 1923 grouping, Great North locomotives bore the brunt of the work on the Buchan, but early in the LNER regime, there were introduced several 4-4-0 tender engines of North British vintage — not 'Scotts' or 'Glens', but of rather humbler station. These seemed to be used more on the Maud to Fraserburgh branch, than on the main line to Peterhead. I can remember frequently seeing, for example, LNER No. 9737 on the Fraserburgh portion of the 5 p.m. ex-Aberdeen. The normal practice was for the Fraserburgh engine to be detached at Maud, and for the Peterhead engine to take both portions on to Aberdeen; but not always. The engine on the 9.07 a.m. ex-Fraserburgh would work through to Aberdeen, taking on the Peterhead coaches at Maud, which I thought was fine, as it gave us from the Broch a sense of superiority over the other lot (See note). I recall yet another variation on the 12.35 p.m. ex-Fraserburgh/12.45 p.m. ex-Peterhead. In that case both engines were seen to surrender at Maud, and the combined load was handed over to a third, appearing whence we knew not. So there must have been a fairly complicated system of locomotive diagramming on the Buchan in those days.

There was a perennial battle against snow. The exposed north-east lowlands of Aberdeenshire have always been prone to severe drifting when onshore winds bring dry snow from the north-east, east or south-east and the numerous cuttings on the Buchan line become ready candidates for blocking. Thus went an old rhyme:

> 'The Buchan train has gaen a stacher,
> She's got snoored up aboot Newmachar,
> May she be spared to rin more swacher,
> In Nineteen hunder an seeven!'

Probably the last big blockage in the cutting north of Newmachar Station will turn out to have been in the great blizzard of 19th January 1960 when the second morning train from Fraserburgh and Peterhead, composed of two d.m.u. twin sets, with about fifty passengers, was obliged to spend twenty-four hours, or thereby, awaiting rescue. That day, nothing much could move, by road or rail, anywhere in the north-east.

From somewhere near this cutting you can see from the train, the Mither Tap of Benachie, and the first time I spotted it, I thought it remarkable to see the familiar landmark from such a distance. In those days, we tended to divide the country into areas served by specific railway lines, and so the whole ribbon from Parkhill to Peterhead was all of a piece — all Buchan. Anywhere on that route was as different from any place in the Garioch as chalk was from cheese. Thus the child's vision of Benachie was a view of home from a strange land across a wide gulf in distance and in everything else.

(Note: In the end, British Railways made Fraserburgh the main line and Peterhead the branch!)

The crew of an ex-LMSR 2P 4-4-0, abandon their charge to seek help
in severe snowstorm conditions near Newmachar in the 1950s.

PETERHEAD STATION

From *The Howes o' Buchan* by William Anderson, editor of the
Peterhead Sentinel, published in 1865

'The station buildings, which stand on the property of the Feuars of
Peterhead, at the west end of Queen Street, are by no means presenting-
looking erections, although durable enough and substantial in their build.
The passenger station, for its size, is a very well-laid-off and commodious
place, having a platform upwards of five hundred feet in length. On a smaller
scale, of course, we have in our station at Peterhead, all the advantages and
facilities possessed in the large terminal stations in the south. The space is
divided thus:- luggage room, guard's room and closet, store-room, stationmaster's room, ticket office, gentlemen's waiting-room, ladies' waiting-room,
boiler room, lamp room and water-closets. A few yards to the south of the
passenger station is erected the carriage shed, a long and somewhat unshapely
wooden building, but well enough fitted for its purpose — that of holding
spare carriages. Then we have the goods station, the arrangement and build of
which is all that could be wished for. Beside the goods station stands the
engine house and water tank, the water for the supply of which is brought all
the way from Howe o' Buchan. The water is forced up by two powerful
'rams' (the design and work of Mr White, coppersmith, Peterhead), to the top
of the brae on the old road overlooking Blackhouse, in order to give it sufficient fall. The 'rams' are well worthy of the inspection of the mechanically
curious'.

Peterhead Station and yard. To the left is the engine shed and the goods
shed is in the centre background. To the right of the goods shed is the
passenger station with an L M S R 2P 4-4-0 departing.

N. R. Knight

A view from Windmill Brae of Peterhead Station in 1890.
Courtesy Frasers Studio, Peterhead

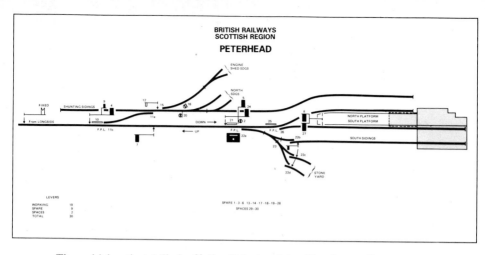

British Railways Scottish Region — Peterhead

The vehicles that killed off the Peterhead to Aberdeen rail passenger traffic. The road route to Aberdeen is fifteen miles shorter than the rail route and the pioneer bus service, first seriously to challenge the railway, was run by Peterhead businessman, James Sutherland. So serious were the inroads made into the traffic, that Sutherland received a deputation of senior LNER directors who offered to buy out Sutherland's bus line. Sutherland's reply was to take his cheque book from his pocket and say, 'How much do you want for your line?'. The LNER retired defeated and passenger traffic remained at a low ebb from Peterhead until final closure of passenger services in 1965.

Courtesy Frasers Studios, Peterhead

An aerial view of Peterhead, taken in 1950. A long freight train can be seen approaching the station.

G.N.S.R.A. Collection

TICKET STORIES
one of an occasional series
by
A. W. Coutts

It was a warm summer's morning as A.F.C. and his family hurried down an already busy Union Street, Aberdeen, in order to catch the 6.55 a.m. train to Fraserburgh. This morning, A.F.C. was going to Fraserburgh to stay with the wife's folk for the weekend. The whole family was draped out in its Sunday best for here was an event warranting such splendour. This was the 'holiday'. Sweating, in the pale, yet warm morning glow of the sun, the family eventually boarded their train, at platform 11, of course, and waited for the punctual departure of their train, for this was GNS practice, all trains ran to time.

Soon a shriek sang shrilly over the docile, dormant Denburn Valley and they were off. As she steamed out of the 'Joint' and up to Kittybrewster, A.F.C. could just hear the clicking of the rail joints and they sped north. With a Cowan's Class 'C' locomotive hauling him towards his destination, he seemed sure of a swift and speedy arrival. The whole family, children and all, began to slumber as the sun rose higher into the morning sky.

Suddenly all were awakened by the sound of escaping steam, and looking out of the window, they found, to their amazement, that they were sitting in Auchnagatt Station and the sound which they were hearing was coming from a Class 'V' locomotive on a southbound train. The train continued on towards Fraserburgh passing Maud Junction where a Class 'R' 0-4-4T locomotive was surprisingly marshalling waggons. A.F.C. sighed as he gazed on the familiar green of the Great North for he had travelled for many years about the

An ex-NBR 4-4-0 is pictured at Maud Station (circa 1937) with a freight from Fraserburgh.

G.N.S.R.A. Collection

system and, in his mind, he considered it to be 'his railway'. On through Strichen the train raced, making up for the time invariably lost at Maud, and into Fraserburgh.

The station was filled with people waiting for the arrival of the 9 a.m. from Aberdeen and the departure of the 9.25 a.m. to that city. A.F.C. quickly ushered his family out of the station, only stopping to glance at the engine shed containing more of the GNS locomotives. He sighed yet again, in his own inimitable style and quickly passed on. His weekend had begun.

A view of Fraserburgh Station in 1910, with the Aberdeen train about to leave. The St. Combs branch train is in the far platform. Of particular interest is the open wagon for the carriage of fish, which can be seen between the locomotive and the coaches.

G.N.S.R.A. Collection

The Earl of Aberdeen's Railway
by
Lord Haddo

My grandfather was a very rich man when he married in 1877. He owned some 60,000 acres which stretched from New Deer to the bridge over the railway at Udny Station and from the Boat of Ardlethen to Crichie. He was determined to build this railway all on his own property which he proposed in 1880. I see the plans are marked 'For Session 1880' and I presume that it would be submitted to Parliament in that year. William Paterson was the Engineer.

The route swirled about avoiding ditches and avoiding over-bridges as much as possible. In the plan quite a few roads would have had to be diverted to avoid too much of a skew on the bridges. The first station is at Cairnbrogie, then Tarves Station, Keithfield Station and a lovely straight bit downhill to a terminus at Methlick.

My grandfather always told me that when the Great North mooted the Buchan line, they were going to come to Udny (Cultercullen in those days), to Pitmedden, Tarves, Methlick, New Deer and then to Maud. My great-great-grandfather, who was a very distinguished politician, is alleged to have had an allergy to new fangled things and would not allow the railway on the estate at all. So that meant it had to turn right at Udny to avoid his property and skirted it all the way down to Ellon and then on to Maud. It was a bad effort by my great-great-grandfather and my grandfather was determined to rectify matters.

I have no plans of the stations and the layouts; no details of costs. I only have the gradient profile and the plans. I suggest we take an imaginary run along the line.

At Udny Station, we would have to change. The actual point of divergence is shown on the plan and at that point I nearly came to a sudden end under the Formartine and Buchan tour as I had hoped the train was going to stop at the point of divergence and had placed myself accordingly, but the train swept by. We turn left here at 1 in 70 by Newcraig Farm, up over the public road at 1 in 76, past Tillymaud, which is about a mile, then down for ½ mile at 1 in 100 to the Denend road, then 1 in 400 for two miles which must have been very dull. We then go down still to Milltown of Coullie and Udny village, now Udny Green, at 1 in 160 for three furlongs.

Leaving Tarves, we go down past Nethermill of Tillyhilt at 1 in 60 for 1,130 yards which includes quite a reasonable curve. Here, there is a deep cut burn and I think there would be quite a little viaduct. This is 7 miles from Udny. Now we go down past Wedderlairs at 1 in 60 for 600 yards to Keithfield Station which is 1 in 330 for 300 yards.

From Keithfield we descent past Courtstone at 1 in 60 for 500 yards to the Keithfield Burn and up past Chapelpark Farm at 1 in 120 for six furlongs. Finally, we go down a lovely straight at 1 in 60, unfortunately, for only six furlongs. We could have probably whacked up quite a reasonable speed. Then past Crimondhill and swinging round left-handed to a terminus at Methlick where, believe it or not, it was level for two furlongs.

The total length was 10 miles 4 furlongs and 1 chain.

My grandfather told me that he thought it was going to cost £80,000. If you remember how much railway estimates rose to incredible heights, you realise it would really have been much more.

I have an illuminated addresss here presented by the tenantry to my grandfather in 1881.

'When in the autumn of last year your Lordship announced the intention of constructing at your sole expense a railway through the lands of Methlick and Tarves to Udny, the primary object of the undertaking being, as we well know, to benefit your tenants, we hail with joy the munificent liberality thus manifested on our behalf. The completion of the costly scheme, thus projected, would have been, we cheerfully acknowledge, of great advantage to the agricultural interests and general business requirements of that portion of your estates; but, when for reasons we fully appreciate, your Lordship deemed it wise to abandon this scheme, and in lieu of that boon, spontaneously intimated entire remission of the current half-year's rent over the whole of your estates, no words of ours can adequately express the feelings of thankfulness which animated us and our families'.

They did things in a grand way in those days. I think it was an awful decision not to build the railway.

I could see the GNSRA joining *Gordon Highlander* between Methlick and Udny and who knows we might have enticed an 'A4' or even a 'City'. However, these are castles in the air and instead, we still have a very contented tenantry.

The railway would have been a tremendous boon to the Estate during the two Wards because we could have loaded our timber at Methlick instead of taking it to Ellon or Aberdeen. It would have suited me well for coming to meetings in Aberdeen, as I could have stepped into a nice warm comfortable train instead of having to drive in a car in all weathers.

TICKET STORIES
one of an occasional series
by
Alan H. Sangster

J. L. had just completed his first week's work as an apprentice stonemason at the quarries in Persley. It was a warm sunny Saturday afternoon as he made his way to Persley Station and his head was full of thoughts of his home at Auchnagatt and his mother's home-made oatcakes and brose. J. L. knocked at the ticket window which was opened by a porter with an enormous walrus moustache; 'Weel, laddie', said the porter in a gruff voice that matched his appearance; 'A third class ticket to Auchnagatt, please', said J. L. with some apprehension.

'Auchnagatt, Auchnagatt', exclaimed the old porter, 'Min, I've nay printed tickets te that place; if I've a fare in my book I'll write een oot, otherwise ye'll hiv te re-book at Dyce'. Luckily a fare was available and J. L. was handed his ticket for which he was charged two shillings and eleven pence. J. L. sat on the platform seat and awaited the arrival of his train which was at 6.36 p.m. A number of trains flashed by during his wait and J. L. thought what wonderful engines the 'Great North' had.

Dead on time the 6.25 p.m. subby from Aberdeen rumbled into the station and J. L. hurriedly boarded the train amid the hiss of steam and slamming of carriage doors as people joined and left the train. With a sharp toot on the engine whistle, the train pulled out of Persley and galloped on to Bucksburn, the next stop.

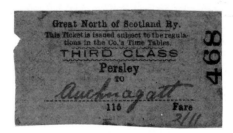

AUCHNAGATT

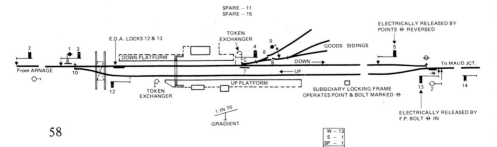

THE STATION, AUCHNAGATT 59766

Auchnagatt Station.

G.N.S.R.A. Collection.

J. L. picked up a newspaper that someone had left in the compartment and noted with joy that the end of the Great War was in sight. Soon, he thought, his elder brother could come home from France where he was serving with the Gordon Highlanders.

In what seemed no time at all, the train was clattering into Dyce. J. L. alighted and watched with fascination as engine No. 86 was uncoupled and ran round the coaches ready to form the 7.00 p.m. back to Aberdeen.

At 7.19 p.m., locomotive No. 55 clanked into the station with the 7.00 p.m. train from Aberdeen for Fraserburgh and Peterhead. J. L. found himself a corner seat in a well upholstered compartment and settled down for the remainder of the journey to Auchnagatt. Parkhill, Newmachar, Udny, Esslemont, Ellon; stops had been made at all of these stations and as the train jolted to a halt at the tiny station of Arnage, J. L. begaon to wonder if he would see home that night as, indeed, since leaving Dyce, his journey had been at a snail's pace. J. L. noted an Aberdeen-bound train standing in the up loop and noted the engine number as 110. After a brief halt at Arnage, the train rattled on towards Auchnagatt. It was almost 8.14 p.m. and J. L. thought how it had taken him almost two hours for the 24 mile journey.

J. L. felt the brakes being applied as the train slowed for its stop at Auchnagatt. He leaned out of the compartment door window and could see a long goods train bound for Kittybrewster standing in the up loop at Auchnagatt Station. The train ground to a halt and J. L. jumped on to the platform and dashed towards his father who had come to meet him. The two men were so engrossed in excited chatter as they left the station, that they failed to notice the hand of the booking clerk held out in vain for J. L.'s ticket. By the time the poor clerk had collected his wits, the two men had boarded a horse and trap and were out of earshot.

As the horse and trap neared the farmhouse, J. L. thought of his journey on the Great North of Scotland Railway and of the waiting feast of home-made oatcakes and a bowl of brose.

THAT WAS LENABO – THAT WAS!

(This article is reproduced by permission of Mr Peter D. Strachan, the *Buchan Observer*, Peterhead and of the author, Mr I. Wilkinson)

Rome was not built in a day. And neither was Lenabo. The Romans took decades; in a comparative jiffy, Lenabo arose from a desolate and hitherto back o' beyond peat bog, flanked by the parishes of Longside and Cruden. The creation of 'Metropolitan Lenabo' was quite a feat.

Fifty years ago the hamlet of Kinmundy witnessed a gigantic earthquake on its doorstep. The moss was alive with toiling humanity, with all the paraphernalia of mechanical excavation belching smoke. Indeed, it is said that a pall still hovers over the district at certain seasons. The scene, viewed from a distance in the twilight, was almost reminiscent of what Dante's 'Inferno' must have been.

An army of navvies – Irish and Scottish – was digging, digging, – under the grey skies of winter and in the flickering light of naptha flares. Thousands of tons of dank peat went into wagons to be dumped, and hundreds more helped to feed the boilers of steam scoops, bucket cranes and locomotives, which ran hither and thither on rails, up hill and down dale, across a site where several smallholdings formerly pursued a precarious livelihood. To house the influx of navvies, huts were erected for sleeping and eating, and there was a 'wet' canteen, with extra police at Longside in case of contingencies.

In the cold, bleak, winter of 1915, it was a hard day's night at Lenabo. 'Blood, sweat and tears' would not too strongly sum it up. Messrs. Tawse, of Aberdeen, to whom the transformation of Lenabo was entrusted, had a tearing, wearing, helter-skelter race against time, for the Government, with the U-boat menace in mind, was insistent that the 'gasbags' on Lenabo RNAS should be operational by the autumn. This meant that the site had to be ready for building to begin by the early summer at least. It was a tribute to the firm's organization, deployment of labour, and the equipment then available, that they were able to complete the task to schedule.

To transport people and material to the scene of operations required the services of a charioteer. Who else but Jimmy Sutherland? With Longside as the railhead for Lenabo, the intervening three or four miles, over a narrow water-bound road, had to be bridged. To do so, Jimmy considerably augmented his fleet of horse-drawn carts and lorries, and there was a constant stream of laden and unladen vehicles between the two points from dawn to dusk. Supplies from Peterhead, rather longer in mileage than the Longside route, were conveyed by steam wagons. It was not until later that the GNSR constructed the branch railway from Longside to Lenabo.

With the site prepared, water and drainage installed, roads constructed, foundations laid on for the giant hangars, ancillary buildings and living quarters, the steel riggers and bricklayers went into action. There was nothing shoddy or flimsy about Lenabo. Only the best was good enough. After all, it was costing a fabulous amount then. Some said £500,000, which would mean about a million sterling today (1965). Amidst the forest of trees you can still spot (if you have permission), the remains of neat brickwork and the massive depth of the concrete foundations.

So up they went, brick upon brick, to emerge in trim avenues, leading from a main entrance, adorned with pseudo-classical pillars, encrusted in concrete. A powerhouse, a gasworks, (to provide helium bouyancy for the airships), a waterworks, steam generators for the hangars, engineering shops, wireless station, canteens, church, cinema, messes, living quarters, garages, and a fire station, nearly all solid stuff of Cruden brick, calculated to survive until eternity, and the whole surrounded by a high spiked steel fence, like an ancient monument. Across the road, on the Kinmundy Estate, was a tiny general store and post office, which managed to cope with unprecedented custom by service through the window and the installation of an outsize letter box.

When complete, Lenabo was a sizeable township, with a population of 500 or so, mainly ratings, engineers and riggers. The operational crews came later. But first to build the 'gasbags'. The framework for these was delivered in pre-fabricated sections and put together in the hangars. An overcoat of silvery grey rubber fabric protected the frame and the gasbag inside. Gondolas were attached, motors (of French manufacture) installed, as well as guns, wireless, various instruments, an anchor and ballast, (this was important). These ships were of the SS and NS types and each hangar accommodated two. The operational distance was limited. They were tricky to handle even in calm weather, and a nightmare in moderate winds. Because the bouyancy upthrust was so strong, it took over a hundred ratings, grasping ropes, to hold a ship to the ground in normal conditions.

There were several incidents in which Lenabo 'gasbags' got out of control. One particularly comes to mind. It was in 1917, when an NS ship, passing over Peterhead, experienced a motor failure. In attempting to lose height, by expelling gas, and land on the Smith Embankment, the ship was slightly damaged by contact with the weathercock on the Town House spire. The landing was achieved with the aid of spectators, who thronged the embankment and clutched the trailing ropes until lorry loads of ratings arrived from Lenabo.

Lenabo's first Commandant was a Royal Marines Officer, Colonel Robinson, and his operational crews were nearly all pioneer aviators of the Royal Navy. Their task was to patrol the near waters of the North Sea as U-boat spotting auxiliaries to the fleet at Peterhead. In the light of history, Lenabo's contribution to U-boat destruction seems to have been negligible, and indeed it lost one ship (its salvaged propeller is in St. John's Church, Longside), in a showdown with a U-boat.

However unspectacular its contribution to the war effort, Lenabo did scintillate as a social asset in a rather moribund hinterland of Buchan. On the station there was abundant talent, and it found an outlet in theatricals, concerts and garden fetes in aid of worthy charities. The station sports day saw Buchan in gala mood, with hospitality and every conceivable amenity laid on, and a hearty welcome for all comers. That there was also some literary distinction at Lenabo was apparent in the column of *The Gasbag* the station's monthly magazine, printed by Peter Scrogie, Peterhead, although it is doubtful if any copies survive.

The branch railway was not completed until 1916, and was used for passengers and goods until 1920. There were two unattended level crossings — across the Peterhead to Banff turnpike and across the Kinmundy road. The turnpike crossing was the scene of a fatality, when of the very few Peterhead motorists, a businessman was killed in collision with a locomotive. The track and earthworks of the branch can still be traced, although now intersected by fences and ditches. Major Hutchison of Cairngall, proprietor of the land through which the line meandered, was paid £2,500 compensation for the wayleave, and he often told the story of how, a few months after receiving the cheque, he had a further one for the same amount, with an identical covering letter. When he returned the second cheque and explained the situation, his honesty received a jolt — there was stony silence!

Until the Armistice, Lenabo was in full sail, and on 11th November 1918, it was a dispatch-rider from thence who brought the official wireless news to the *Buchan Observer* office, for publication in the Special Armistice Edition of that paper. In the following year, when the coal strike suspended many rail services, Lenabo helped maintain postal traffic between Peterhead and Aberdeen with Crossley motor wagons. It was in that year, too, that the RAF came into being and succeeded the RNAS at Lenabo. With the war at an end, there was nothing to do except continue essential services and spit and polish. The station served no useful purpose and was unsuitable for winged aircraft training. Demobilisation reduced its complement to skeleton proportions and, in 1920, the Air Ministry withdrew and wiped Lenabo off its map. It was relegated to the Disposals Board.

Visionaries hereabouts saw in Lenabo a magnificent, ready-made industrial potential. Our proposal was to use it for large-scale peat processing; another was a canning factory, with Messrs. Ritchie mass-producing their prime ox-tongues and a canned vegetable sideline. Yet another was to create a pastoral precint, and call it 'New Kinmundy'. The visionaries (who, by the way, nearly all sported silver grey waterproof coats, made from the dismantled airship fabric) received no official support. There were no 'takers', and a short-sighted County Council was no more interested then than it was when such admirable assets as Pitfour and the Cruden Bay Hotel came crashing down. So Lenabo was sold to the demolition contractors for a song. But not the site. It had belonged to the old Keith domain of Ludquharn which, in turn, was part of the Aden Estate, and it was said that Aden received £5,000 for the freehold of Lenabo. For long, the site lay derelict, until it was offered to the Forestry Commission, which has restored to a petrified forest a bountiful and fairyland garland of sylvan beauty.

Dr. Emslie corresponded with Mr Iain Wilkinson, the author of the above article, about Lenabo and extracts of the correspondence are reproduced below:

The line (Longside—Lenabo) was some 2½ miles in length, had no signals (apart from one at Longside Junction), and no terminal build-ings. It left the Maud—Peterhead branch east of Longside Station, traversed the Estate of Cairngall, the main Peterhead—Banff turnpike thence in the direction of Kinmundy, crossing the public road there and entering the precincts of Lenabo at Savoch (I think). Flanking the Kinmundy road was a terminal, with platform and a couple of sidings. This line was not part of the original Lenabo plan; it was an after-thought. The transport facilities were provided, mainly, by James Sutherland, horse-master, Peterhead, who used horse carts and lorries and a few steam lorries and trucks to convey men and materials to the site (where several hundred navvies had quarters). It was half a century ago this year that the GNSR began construction of the railway, which was completed within a few months. Its course can still be followed although the embankments, and culverts are ruinous in places (indeed non-existent where farming and ditching operations have intervened). I don't think the trestle bridge is there now.

The branch was used for passenger as well as goods traffic. Passenger traffic comprised drafts of naval ratings who were sometimes accommo-dated in through carriages off south trains at Aberdeen or changed into the 'Lenabo Special' (usually one antiquated coach), which often had attached vans and trucks containing supplies. There was one fatal accident at the Peterhead—Banff crossing. One would have thought that tank locomotives would have been more suited to a short almost level route. But no! Manson 4-4-0s, often running tender first (hence the fatality) were used.

Only Service personnel used the line. It is the case that Messrs. Tawse constructed the earthworks, culverts and bridge; GNSR permanent way gangers laid the track. I don't recall that 0-4-0 tanker. Perhaps it was hired to or belonged to Tawse, who used one or two locos on the site of the airship base. It was always the ubiquitous 4-4-0 I saw, sometimes tender first. I think the safety precautions at the crossings were very casual. The Peterhead couple involved in the smash were the subject of a 'Fatal Accidents Inquiry', reported in the press at that time. The then station agent at Longside, (Birnie), was quite a character, but like so many others who might have proved useful informants, he's gone.

As for the base itself, it was built on a back-o'-beyond peat bog, the property of the Aden Estate. Early in 1915 the Admiralty engaged Messrs. Tawse to prepare the site, lay foundations, construct a waterworks, drainage and roads, and erect certain ancillary buildings; other contractors and the Admiralty itself built the two airship sheds and installed machinery and various services. Most of the living quarters, powerhouse, gasworks, church, cinema and canteens were constructed of Cruden brick, transported to the site over the moss road from Hatton by steam wagons. It was a rush job and was so far completed to enable occupation by the Royal Naval Air Service, as an airship station, in the late autumn of 1915, although it wasn't entirely operational until the summer of 1916. The station was controlled operationally by the Rear Admiral of Peterhead. In 1919 the base was declared redundant and sold to Brands, of Dundee, for demolition, which was completed in 1920—21.

Hatton, with its station, 1905.

Courtesy Frasers Studios, Peterhead

THE PETERHEAD QUARRY RAILWAY

(The following article is based on one which appeared in the *Locomotive Magazine*, for May 1900. At that time it was the only British State Railway, hence the title of the original article, *A British State Railway* by R.S.H.A.G.F.)

In 1884, the Admiralty commenced the construction of a gigantic breakwater across Peterhead Bay to convert it into a harbour secure in all weathers. The total cost of the undertaking was estimated at £750,000 and it was anticipated that the work would last until 1920. The granite used in the concrete is excavated, by convict labour from Peterhead Prison, from a quarry on Stirling Hill about two miles from the works and prison. When the British Government undertake any work one may, as a rule, depend upon that work being well done, so to convey the convicts to and from the quarries and the granite to the breakwater, an elaborate little railway was constructed.

Although the total length of the line was but 2½ miles, the whole works were of the most elaborate construction; heavy flat-bottomed rails weighing about 72 lb per yard and spiked to the sleepers in the ordinary manner to form the permanent way, which was firmly and compactly ballasted with granite. The line contained some engineering works of fair size, including a massive viaduct of several spans of granite masonry, a steel girder bridge across the turnpike road, two masonry overbridges and heavy cuttings and embankments. In general equipment, too, this railway was fully equal to a trunk line, being provided with a complete signalling system, all trains being worked on the absolute block from three cabins in electrical communication with each other.

Early stages of construction of the south arm of Admiralty Breakwater (Peterhead), 1891.

65

Courtesy Frasers Studios, Peterhead

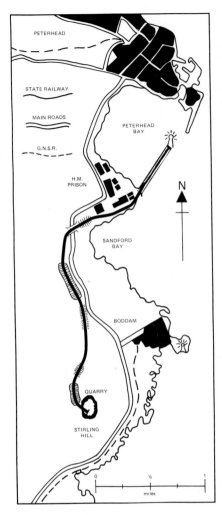

The passenger train service consisted of two trains in each direction daily for the conveyance of the convicts and the officers travelling to their work. These trains left Admiralty Station, Peterhead, at 7.15 a.m. and 1.00 p.m., and from Stirling Hill at 11.00 a.m. and 5.00 p.m. Mineral trains were run as required for conveying granite to the work, the wagons used for this traffic being of steel. Four corridor cars comprised the passenger stock. These coaches were of very substantial construction, and were more remarkable for utility than comfort. Each ran on four wheels, and was divided by longitudinal partitions into six compartments opening off a transverse corridor in the centre of the car. There were no windows in the compartment, but there were the usual ones in the side doors. Each coach carried 30 to 35 passengers, and a train usually about 100.

The locomotives were four in number, six-coupled tank engines, *Victoria* (1892), *Prince of Wales* (1892), *Alexandra* (1892) and *Duke of York* (1896). The latter three were built by the Hunslet Engine Company, Leeds; the dimensions were: cylinders, 15 in. by 20 in.; diameter of drivers, 3 ft. 4 in.; wheelbase, 10 ft. 3 in.; heating surface, 706 sq. ft.; grate area, 10½ sq. ft.; weight in working order, 28¾ tons. *Victoria*, built by Messrs. Hawthorn, Leslie & Co. Newcastle, had similar dimensions, but was an outside connected saddle tank. All four were painted dull olive green, and had polished brass domes. There were no continuous brakes in use. A wagon was placed at the front of the train for the convenience of occasional passengers, these not being permitted in the convict cars.

THE PETERHEAD QUARRY RAILWAY – AGAIN
by
John A N. Emslie

In the May 1971 issue of the *Review*, pages 155 and 156, there was reprinted an article describing the railway which once linked Stirlinghill Quarry, near Boddam, with the prison and breakwater to the south of Peterhead. Additional information has come to hand about this unusual line which amplifies, and amends, some of the earlier statements.

Several years ago I wrote to the Director of the Prison and Borstal Services, Scottish Home and Health Department, to enquire about the history of the 'prison railway'. The reply I received contained the following statements:

> 'The prison land was purchased in July 1885 for £5,000 and schedules and specifications for the building of the prison issued in 1886. The prison was opened on 8th August 1888 and by March 1891 all the cells for convicts, it was then intended to provide, had been nearly completed. Convict labour started work in the Admiralty Yard in 1889 under an engineer in charge of construction of a breakwater to form the harbour of refuge.
>
> On the subject of the railway in its later years, all I have been able to discover is that under the direction of a Civil Engineer, Colonel Littlejohn, (since retired), who was employed by the Admiralty who operated and maintained the railway, the uplifting and disposal of the lines, coupled with the dismantling and breaking up of the four locomotives, spread over a period of approximately eight years, from 1950 to 1958. It would appear that all the records held by Colonel Littlejohn were sent to London and obviously these records would provide you with the information required'.

From this it is clear that the railway was not really a prison or quarry railway but was the Peterhead Harbour of Refuge Railway – a distinctly Admiralty operation. It construction would have taken place about 1887 or 1888 but the article in the *Locomotive Magazine* of 1900, reprinted in the *Review*, was too early to include mention of a second line which served the building of a north breakwater on the other side of the bay from the prison, and close to the town of Peterhead. There, about 1910, an entirely separate set of tracks was laid and an engine shed provided, although, like the original line, this too did not connect in any way with GNSR metals.

On 22nd September 1949, Mr H. D. Bowtell, visited the two systems and met the Admiralty's Resident Engineer, Col. Littlejohn, and the Foreman Mr Flett. The following notes made by Mr Bowtell are of interest:

Peterhead Prison Railway locomotive, *Edward VII.*

B. J. Ritchie

Alexandra	0-6-0T, side tanks: Hunslet Engine Co. No. 548 of 1891; 3ft. 4in. diameter driving wheels; 15in. by 20in. cylinders, inside frames. (Spare on that day, inside shed at prison).
Duke of York	0-6-0T, side tanks: Hunslet Engine Co. No. 644 of 1896; 3ft. 4in. diameter driving wheels; 15in. by 20in. cylinders, inside frames. (Also in shed at prison).
Edward VII	0-6-0T, side tanks: Hawthorn Leslie No. 2614 of 1905; 3ft. 6in. diameter driving wheels; 14in. by 22in. cylinders, outside frames. (In steam at prison shed – this locomotive had been on loan to Rosyth Admiralty Dockyard, Fife, some time during the 1939–45 War).
Prince of Wales	0-6-0T, side tanks: Hunslet Engine Co. No. 559 of 1892; 3ft. 4in. diameter driving wheels: 15in. by 20in. cylinders, inside frames. (At work on the north breakwater lines; in green livery – this locomotive had been used by the Admiralty at Lyness, in Orkney, some time during, or just after, World War I and had been returned to Peterhead about 1920).

A fifth locomotive had been broken up about 1935

Victoria	0-6-0T, side tanks: Hawthorn Leslie No. 2138 of 1889; 3ft. 4in. diameter driving wheels; 14in. by 22in. cylinders, outside frames.

(I am indebted to the Scottish Home and Health Department and to Harold Bowtell for the extra information on this relatively little-known line – JE)

LIVESTOCK CHARGES

The following article is from a newspaper cutting which has come into our hands — no date and no name of the newspaper:

'I have now and then raised my voice, so to say, in a tiny newspaper with reference to the sins and shortcomings of the Great North of Scotland Railway Company, and have railed on them in good terms for the exorbitant fares, the slowness of their trains, and the prehistoric character of their stations. I have got much amusement out of their by-laws, one time and another, and I have speculated as to the pains and penalties I should have endured if I were guilty of such a heinous offence as the transfer of one of their 'non-transferable' tickets. If the Company carried humans by avoirdupois scale as they do cattle and pigs, I could understand, in a dim way, why they objected to ticket transfer; but as they don't, and make no more charge for a 24 stone giant than they do for a 7 stone pigmy, the true inwardness of the non-transferable ticket by-law passes my poor comprehension. But that is not the only railway mystery. There are mysteries of goods and live-stock traffic just as there are mysteries of passenger traffic, and before me, as I write, I have the letter of a friend containing a new and heart-breaking conundrum, which he wishes me to assist him in solving. Stated briefly, the puzzle might be thus put — 'If 2 live pigs in one box, weighing 3 cwt., cost 10s 10d carriage from Cruden Bay to Kittybrewster, what ought to be the current retail price of pork sausages'? Manifestly this is a case for the employment of logarithms, the infinitesimal calculus, and the Babbage machine.

Needless to say, my friend is not interested in regard to the retail price of sausages; it is the monstrous charge of 10s 10d carriage for 3 cwts. of live pig from Cruden Bay to Kittybrewster that is disturbing his mind, and no wonder. It would have been money in my friend's pocket to have sent the swine as first class passengers, had it been possible to persuade the Great North of Scotland Railway officials that swine might be thus carried — which, as Euclid says, is absurd. But it is really not more absurd than 10s 10d carriage for two pigs, a distance of 25 miles odd. And how the Company would proceed to demonstrate the reasonableness of the charge, I have no more notion than the man in the moon, and therefore, I have great pleasure in giving up any attempt at a solution, and in throwing the whole onus of the proof on the Railway Company. But the worst of it is that my friend propounds other abstruse puzzles of railway rates, and, disregarding the fact that I am struggling with a problem of my own — how to cure a persistent influenza — he asks me to work out, by geometric scale, or by algebraic symbol, the following additional brainwrecker:- 'If a certain class of empties are carried from Aberdeen to Cruden Bay at 3d per cwt., what should the rate be from Ellon to Cruden Bay? Simple proportion to the simple minded would bring the rate out in the region of a penny or thereabouts, but the railway arithmetic gives the answer 'sevenpence'! which is an outrage on free elementary education.

Tullochgorum

ST. COMBS BRANCH LINE
by
W.R.S.

I take strong exception to Cairnbulg being listed as an obvious halt, unable to deal with carriages and motors maybe, as there was no dock platform for end loading. But it was a station from its inception in 1903 until BR withdrew all the staff in 1960 when tickets were issued on the trains by the guard. Using the modern idiom, these are now termed 'pay trains'.

The building of the St. Combs branch was completed and the line opened to traffic on 1st July 1903. It was a 'Light Railway' during its lifetime, approximately five miles in length from its own platform number 3 at Fraserburgh to the terminus at St. Combs. Intermediately it served Kirkton Bridge Halt, adjacent to Fraserburgh Golf Club, and Philorth Bridge Halt quite close to Lord Saltoun's seat at Cairnbulg Castle.

Cairnbulg Station, 3½ miles from 'The Broch', served the twin villages of Cairnbulg and Inverallochy. Various tales are told regarding the building of the line, help in labour and money being donated by the householders in Cairnbulg, Inverallochy and St. Combs, and the gift of land from the local lairds. The station to serve the first two villages was intended to be built on Inverallochy land. In fact the first tickets to be issued were from Iverallochy Station, but the Laird of Cairnbulg offered a bigger and more suitable piece of land free, if the station was built on his land. Accordingly, the station stood on Cairnbulg land and took its name from there. A St. Combs resident to this day, Mr A. Cheyne, 6 High Street, worked on the building of the railway and remained on the permanent staff until he retired.

The single line had rounding loops at St. Combs and Cairnbulg, the loop being removed from the latter during my stay there. The driver carried a key, which operated the lock controlling the points. There were no signals except, of course, at Fraserburgh.

Being the last branch line to be opened by the Great North of Scotland Railway Company, it was built to serve the fishing villages of Cairnbulg, Inverallochy and St. Combs. The fishermen and fishwives used the train extensively to carry their fishing gear and fish traffic to and from Fraserburgh. In the days before the Second World War, a good deal of fish was handled at both Cairnbulg and St. Combs, from where it was sent to the market at Fraserburgh. When the inshore men started using Fraserburgh Harbour, this traffic dwindled away. Lobsters and crabs and salmon-netting continued during their respective seasons but the villages became more or less residential in function. The majority of the fishermen followed the herring and seine-net fishing from Fraserburgh. The busiest time of the year was from June to August during the summer herring season at Fraserburgh, but I think the greatest excitement was in November when the crews were returning from the East Anglian herring season, both men and women, who were south, working for curers, coming home with 'kists' full of presents. Many a

LNER Class 'F4', No. 67157, Worsdell's ex-Great Eastern Railway 2-4-2T, stands in Fraserburgh Station in 1952. This locomotive was the last survivor of the class and, along with No. 67164, was fitted with cow-catchers for working the St. Combs branch.

N. R. Knight

Former GER Class 'F4' 2-4-2T, (BR No. 67164) starts to round its train at St. Combs. The cow-catcher was fitted to this locomotive as the line was not fenced. Brackets, for the destination board, can be seen fitted to the smoke-box door. The vehicles behind the locomotive are also of particular interest.

G.N.S.R.A. Collection

Class 'F4', No. 67157, complete with cow-catcher, awaits departure from St. Combs with a motley collection of coaches for Fraserburgh in 1952.

N. R. Knight

St. Combs Station, 25th January 1964.

C. Gammell

Christmas stocking was filled with the 'goodies' brought home from Yarmouth or Lowestoft. It was during the festive season that the 'Annual Walks' were held. Headed by their flute band, the villagers dressed in their Sunday best, visited the neighbouring villages. Inverallochy was the first off, with their march on Christmas Day, followed by Cairnbulg on New Year's Day. The St. Combs folk, or the 'New Towners' as they were called, held their walk on Auld Eel's Day (5th January). This was a time of great feasting and a big dinner was the order of the day after the walk. In the afternoon the children were entertained and in the evening it was the turn of the adults to fill the hall at the annual soirees.

Being an incomer, I used to be amused at the friendly rivalry between the three villages. More so, I think, between Cairnbulg and Inverallochy. Of the local services, Inverallochy claimed post office, school and church, where on Sundays, the 'Bulgers' occupied the Cairnbulg pews on one side and on the other side the Inverallochy pews were filled with 'Cottoners'. This demarcation was carried to the last resting place of all, in Cairnbulg ground where the centre path divided the two. I am told, that St. Peter must have demanded a compromise as the cemetery is now known under the joint names of both places.

One may claim that there was a connection between the station and the cemetery, in addition to sharing the same name. For a year or two after I went there, the LNER ran funeral trains from the station to Philorth Bridge Halt, adjacent to the cemetery. The train used was the 1.40 p.m. (ordinary) St. Combs to Fraserburgh and after arrival at Fraserburgh returned to the halt to convey the mourners back to Cairnbulg Station. When these trains were withdrawn, the rounding loop, previously mentioned, was lifted. It is not known for what purpose this loop was laid at Cairnbulg, however, it did serve a real need when Fraserburgh airfield was built at the beginning of the 1939—45 War. A daily freight service was run from Fraserburgh with building materials and, after completion, a considerable amount of goods was handled during the time the RAF was there. I well remember the day near the end of the war when the driver of the 1.45 p.m. (we were not continental then) from St. Combs stopped on approach to Cairnbulg when he observed a low flying aircraft coming in over the North Sea. It was a 'Jerry' with six of 'Goering's angels', who gave themselves up on landing. It was rumoured that they absconded from Norway.

The St. Combs branch met a real need in transporting the people and their goods during a few decades, shrugging off the challenge of the more flexible bus, than many another branch or main line. The St. Combs inhabitants, unlike their Inverallochy and Cairnbulg cousins, had 'Hobsons's Choice'. The local bus was never able to get a wheel in there.

The famous doctor changed all that, during his stay at the helm. The line has gone, the stations and halts have been razed to the ground and, when visiting old friends, it is sad to see the station house at Cairnbulg standing derelict, its windows boarded up. A grim reminder indeed of present day progress.

Ex-GNSR 4-4-0 *Benachie* (BR No. 62274) shunts fish vans at Fraserburgh on 15th August 1955.

E. C. Haywood

FISH ON THE BUCHAN

The Buchan lines, as recalled elsewhere, did not have any glamorous or special trains such as ran on Deeside. In those days, goods trains were not named and, as on most railways, did not receive much notice from railway authors. Yet it was said that the 'Fish Specials' earned the 'saxpences' for the Great North and the shares were known on the Stock Exchange as 'Haddocks'.

Before 1914, the fish traffic was comparatively small; in 1912, about 2,500 tons of fish were carried by the whole system whereas in 1918, 28,500 were sent from Peterhead and Fraserburgh alone. The reason for this striking change was the diversion of the large export trade to Germany and Russia to inland markets, some of which lost their usual sources on the east coast of England. However, when one remembers that this fish traffic was carried on open wagons (OBs) for a short period in the season, extra trains would be run of which only telegraphic notice would be given. The peak of the fish traffic was probably reached in 1918 when, on 2nd July, sixteen special trains ran on the Buchan. In 1920 there was an occasion when fourteen specials ran from Peterhead. The special supplement for July 1918 showed five specials from Fraserburgh and four from Peterhead. This gives some idea of the flexibility of the workings. In 1930, there were specials from Peterhead at 10.15a.m. 11.05a.m. and 2.10p.m.; from Fraserburgh at 10.10a.m., 11.00a.m. and 2.15p.m.; from Maud, made up from wagons worked from Peterhead and Fraserburgh on the passenger trains, at 1.38p.m. and 4.20p.m. Most of the trains were shown as combining at Maud, often

Landing of the 'Silver Darlings' (Herring), with lines of steam drifters in Peterhead Harbour in the early 1900s. Thousands of tons of fish were sent south by rail. Peterhead is now the biggest fishing port in Europe as well as an important oil port.

Courtesy Frasers Studio, Peterhead

A fish train being loaded at Peterhead.

G.N.S.R.A. Collection

Fraserburgh locomotive shed, in 1955, with ex-GNSR 4-4-0, (BR No. 62276). The long wheelbase fish vans can be seen in the passenger station.

A. Sangster Collection

being double-headed from there but arrangements existed for running the train independently. Double-heading was preferable, as it saved line capacity, but its disadvantage was crossing other trains.

All the traffic had to be worked over a single line with crossing places, some of which were not long. Special instructions were issued about the lengths of the trains:

Kittybrewster—Maud . . . . .Maximum length 995 ft.
Maud—Peterhead .Maximum length 869 ft.
Maud—Fraserburgh . . . . .Maximum length 597 ft.

There was an additional restriction on trains which had to cross at Esslemont where the maximum length permitted was 900 ft. As a guide an engine and tender were taken as 53 ft. while the Company's waggons were 20 ft. Care had to be taken with waggons of 'foreign companies' as their length, (of the waggon), varied considerably. To relieve the post 1914—18 bulge of traffic, the line north of Parkhill was doubled for 1 mile 1,197 yards to a new signal box at Elrick and a new loop was put in at Esslemont. The latter loop was brought into use on Sunday, 3rd August 1919, while the double line section was in use from Sunday, 30th May 1920. In October 1921, the three boxes Parkhill, Elrick and Esslemont were temporarily

L&NER FRASERBURGH STATION

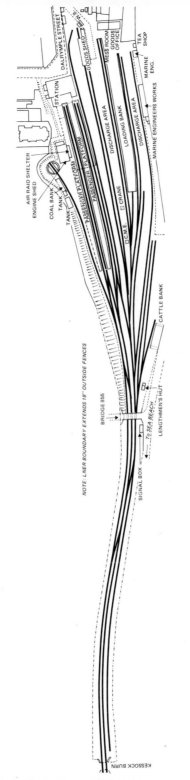

N

SCALE

0 50 100   200   300   400

FEET

NOTE: LNER BOUNDARY EXTENDS 18" OUTSIDE FENCES

DALRYMPLE STREET

GOODS SHED

MESS ROOM
GOODS OFFICE

TEA SHOP

STATION

MARINE ENG.

AIR RAID SHELTER

ENGINE SHED

COAL BANK

TANK

TANK

PASSENGER PLATFORM

PASSENGER 1 PLATFORM

DISCHARGE AREA

LOADING BANK

DISCHARGE AREA

MARINE ENGINEERS WORKS

CRANE

D.C.M.E.

CATTLE BANK

BRIDGE B55

LENGTHMEN'S HUT

To SEA BEACH

SIGNAL BOX

KESSOCK BURN

closed for the winter. They were opened each summer for the season (about May until September or October) until 1925 when they were finally closed. The traffic had fallen to a level which could be worked with the original crossing places.

The diagramming of locomotives must have been quite an art. For the specials in 1930, five specials turns were rostered but there was no mention of the locomotives for the two specials from Maud:

The 4.00 a.m. special from Kittybrewster worked the 11.00 a.m. fish from Fraserburgh:
The 4.23 a.m. ex-Kittybrewster worked the 10.15 a.m. fish from Peterhead:
The 7.13 a.m. ex-Kittybrewster worked the 2.15 p.m. ex-Fraserburgh:
The pilot engine on the 7.13 a.m. ex-Kittybrewster was detached at Maud and went to Peterhead, light engine, to work the fish from there at 11.05 a.m.:
The 10.00 a.m. regular goods was piloted to Maud, whence the engine went light to Peterhead to work the 2.10 p.m. fish:
The engine of the 8.13 a.m. Maud to Fraserburgh, worked the 10.10 a.m. fish to Maud and then returned to Fraserburgh, light engine:

It can be seen that the morning trains were rostered to be combined from Maud and hauled there by one locomotive, while the afternoon trains could be double-headed or run independently from Maud.

A North British diesel-electric locomotive stands at Peterhead Station on 25th January 1964.

C. Gammell

Train Classification	Aberdeen	Kittybrewster	Maud	Fraserburgh	Peterhead
H		4.10 a.m. ——————→		7.47 a.m.	
pass			9.52 a.m. ←——	9.10 a.m.	
LE			10.10 a.m. ——————→		10.36 a.m.
K(SX)		3.48 a.m. ←————————			12.54 p.m.
K(SO)		4.15 a.m. ←————————			12.54 p.m.
H		4.30 a.m. ————————→			8.03 a.m.
pass	10.53 a.m. ←————————				9.25 a.m.
H(SX)		5.55 a.m. ·————————→		9.40 a.m.	
C	1.15 p.m. ←————————			11.23 a.m.	
pass	8.20 a.m. ————————→				10.05 a.m.
C	12.58 p.m. ←————————				11.18 a.m.
H		8.43 a.m. ————————→			11.05 a.m.
C(Q)	4.28 p.m. ←————————				2.30 p.m.
H		9.05 a.m. ————————→		12.21 p.m.	
C(SO)	3.36 p.m. ←————————			1.50 p.m.	
C(SX)	4.08 p.m. ←————————			2.40 p.m.	
K		12.50 p.m. ————————→		5.20 p.m.	
K			9.15 a.m. ←——	7.00 a.m.	
pass			9.37 a.m. —→	10.05 a.m.	
K		7.08 p.m. ←————————		12.50 p.m.	
C	11.38 a.m. ←————————			9.46 a.m.	

(SX) indicates Saturdays excepted
(SO) indicates Saturdays only
(Q) indicates runs when required

The engine for this last turn was almost certainly provided by a northbound pilot working. The brake van for the train was provided from the 4.10 a.m. from Kittybrewster.

The rolling stock has changed; most of the fish was carried in open wagons, sheeted over. There are photographs of these wagons being loaded in a manner similar to the holds of the trawlers which brought in the fish. Fish which had been gutted was boxed, and the boxes stowed in these wagons and sheeted. Now, fish trains are composed of insulated vans, those for the high speed trains to London have roller bearings and a large 'blue spot' for easy identification.

Very little fish is sent by rail; most of it is sent to London, and in connection with the 1.43 p.m. train from Aberdeen there is a train from Fraserburgh arriving in Aberdeen just after 1.00 p.m. While this is a train for freight, most of the traffic is fish for London. Changed days from seeing a train leave the 'Broch' with seven vans, five of them fish, from 1918, when there were seven trains of fish vans in one day!

This article was written before withdrawal of the freight service. No fish train services exist from Aberdeen in the present day, all traffic having been transferred to road.

Special Notices—continued.

12. **FISH TRAFFIC**

The following is a complete Special Time Table of all and the Special Trains for the Fish Traffic, which will have the Ordinary Buchan Trains in the Working Time Tables altered by the following arrangements and notes of working.

DOWN TRAINS.

STATIONS.	Fraserburgh Goods.	Peterhead Goods.	Passenger.	Mail.	Empty Trucks and Waggons at Kittybrewster for Fraserh and Fburgh.	Passenger.	Fraserburgh Goods.	Empty Trucks and Waggons at Kittybrewster for Fraserh and Fburgh.	Saturdays only. Passenger.	Fish on Saturdays. Buchan and Vans.	Passenger.	Peterhead Goods.	Saturdays only. Engine and Van.	Empty Trucks and Waggons at Kittybrewster for Fraserh and Fburgh.	Passenger.
	1	2	3	4	5	6	7	8	9	10	11	12	13	14	15
	a.m.	a.m.	a.m.	a.m.	a.m.	a.m.	a.m.	a.m.	a.m.	a.m.	p.m.	p.m.	p.m.	p.m.	p.m.
Aberdeen, dep.			8 15	9 25		12 20			1 20	2 40	3 50	4 0		4 45	6 45
K'brewster, arr.									1 25		4 0			4 55	
K'brewster, dep.	5 0	5 15	8 19	9 29	9 36	12 24	11 45	1 45	2 45	Stop.	4 4	4 35	Stop.	6 0	6 49
Woodside,			8 22			12 27			2 49		4 7				6 52
Buxburn,			8 26			12 12	8		2 54		4 11				6 57
Dyce, arr.	5 20	5 35	8 31	9 35	9 50	12 36	12 16		2 59		4 19	4 45			7 2
Dyce, dep.	5 25	5 45	8 32	9 36	10 0	12 37	1 2	1 53	3 1		4 19	5 5		6 15	7 3
Parkhill,			8 35			12 40	1 10		3 5		4 24	B			7 6
Newmachar,	5 45	5 58	8 45			12 52	1 28	2 10	3 17		4 38	5 25			7 17
Udny, arr.									3 22						
Udny, dep.	6 0	6 30	8 55	9 53	10 39	1 0	1 45	2 35	3 26		4 50	5 42			7 27
Logierieve,	6 10	6 38	9 0			1 4	1 55		3 31		4 54	C			7 31
Esslemont,	6 20	6 46	9 4			1 8	2 5		3 36		4 57	C			7 35
Ellon, arr.							2 10		3 40						
Ellon, dep.	6 30	7 0	9 11	10 5	10 55	1 15	2 19	2 50	Stop.		5 2	6 5			7 41
Arnage,	6 45	7 25	9 21	10 14		1 24	2 33				5 12	6 27			7 50
Av'nag at arr.							3 22								
Ad'er-	7 5	8 2	9 33	10 23		1 54	2 50	3 27			5 24	6 42			A
Maud, arr.	7 20	8 15	9 45	10 31	11 20	1 42	3 5	3 40			5 35	6 55		7 30	8 10
	M'xd a.m.										Pass. p.m.				
Maud, dep.	8 0		9 58	10 35	12 5	1 45	3 20	3 55			4 29	5 40		7 50	1
Brucklay,	8 10							4 7			4 25	5 44			S
Strichen,	8 28		10 13	10 48		2 0	3 59				4 36	5 55			8 30
Mormond,	8 38		10 19			2 6	4 6				4 41	6 3			8 36
Lonmay,	8 48		10 25	10 59		2 13	4 15				4 50	6 10			8 42
Rathen,	8 56		10 31	11		2 20	4 15				4 56	6 16			8 49
Philorth,															
F'burgh, arr.	9 10		10 40	11 10	12 40	2 30	4 35	4 45			5 5	6 25		8 30	9 0
	Pass. a.m.	G'ds a.m.													
Maud, dep.	8 0	8 25	9 52	10 35	12 0	1 45		3 50			5 40	7 5		7 50	8 15
Mintlaw, arr.												7 20			
Mintlaw, dep.	8 10	8 40	10 1	10 44		1 54		4 2			5 49	7 34			8 24
Longside, arr.															
Longside, dep.	8 18	8 55	10 8	10 51		2 1					5 56	7 47			8 32
Newseat,	8 22		10 12			2 4					6 0				8 38
Inverugie,	8 26	9 5	10 16			2 10					6 5	8 0			8 42
Peterhead, arr.	8 35	9 15	10 25	11 5	12 30	2 20		4 25			6 15	8 10		8 25	8 50

d Stop for crossing purposes only.

Special Notices—continued.

ARRANGEMENTS.

Trains on the Buchan Section, including the Ordinary Trains effect until further notice. The Traffic Working Notes to are to have effect, except in so far as they are superseded or

UP TRAINS.

STATIONS.	Fraserburgh Goods.	Passenger.	Passenger.	Peterhead Goods.	Goods.	Special Fish.	Passenger.	Fish on Saturdays. Special Fish.	Saturdays only. Special Fish.	Goods.	Mail.	Saturdays only. Passenger.	Passenger.	Special Fish.
	1	2	3	4	5	6	7	8	9	10	11	12	13	14	15
	a.m.	a.m.	a.m.	a.m.	a.m.	a.m.	a.m.	p.m.	p.m.	p.m.	p.m.	p.m.	p.m.	p.m.
Peterhead, dep.		7 15	9 20	8 35	9 40	11 5		1 6	1 30	2 20	2 20	3 40		7 10	7 0
Inverugie,		7 20	9 24	8 43	9 50			1 5			3 44			7 15	
Newseat,		7 24						1 10			3 48			7 19	
Longside,		7 30	9 32	8 55	10 8			1 16		2 40	3 53			7 25	
Mintlaw, arr.				9 5											
Mintlaw, dep.		7 39	9 40	9 15	10 17			1 25	1 54		2 55	4 2		7 34	7 20
Maud, arr.		7 45	9 50	9 30	10 25	11 40		1 35	2 5	2 55	3 5	4 11		7 45	7 30
F'burgh, dep.	5 30	7 0	9 10			10 55	10 40	12 50	1 15		2 0	3 35		7 0	6 50
Philorth,															
Rathen,	5 40	7 7	9 16			11 4	10 50	12 58			2 6	3 40		7 7	
Lonmay, arr.							10 59								
Lonmay, dep.	5 52	7 14	9 21			11 20	11 0	1 5			2 13	3 45		7 14	
Mormond,		7 21	9 28			11 29	1 14				2 19	3 50		7 20	
Strichen,		7 28	9 32			11 40	1 21				2 25	3 59		7 29	
Brucklay,		7 35	9 43			11 55	1 32	1 50			2 35			7 40	
Maud, arr.	6 40	7 44	9 59			12 10	1 40	2 0			2 45	4 d		7 45	7 30
Maud, dep.	6 50	7 53	9 56	10 5		11 52	12 15	1 45	2 15	3 10	3 10	4 16		7 50	8 10
uchnagatt,	7 5	8 10		10 23			12 30	1 55		3 22	3 22	4 24		8 0	
Arnage,	7 25	8 10	10 14	10 35			12 45	2 7	2 35	3 43				8 10	
Ellon, arr.							1 0								
Ellon, dep.	7 45	8 20		10 55			1 15	2 19	2 50	3 50	3 58	4 39	7 50	8 20	
Esslemont,	7 55	8 25	10 30				1 25	2 24				7 55	8 25	
Logierieve,	8 7	8 30	10 34				1 33	2 29				8 0	8 30	
Udny, arr.	8 17														
Udny, dep.	8 55	8 35	10 39	11 13			1 45	2 35			4 25	4 50	8 8	8 35	
Newmachar,	9 10	8 45	10 48	11 28		12 52	2 10	2 46			4 38	+	8 15	8 46	
Parkhill,	9 25						2 25	2 57					8 26	8 57	
Dyce, arr.	9 35	8 58	10 58	11 45			2 35	3 1			4 50	5 5	8 29	9 0	
Dyce, dep.	9 42	9 0	11 0	11 50			2 40	3 27	4 15	5 10	5 5	8 30	9 2	
Buxburn,	10 0						2 50	3 7			5 23		8 35	9 7	
Woodside,		9 10	11 10					3 11					8 40	9 11	
K'brewster, arr.															
K'brewster, dep.	10 10	9 15	11 15	12 10			3 20	3 15			5 35	5 15	8 45	9 15	
Aberdeen, arr.	10 20	9 20	11 20	12 15			1 15	3 30	3 20	4 0	4 35	5 40	5 20	8 50	9 20	9 30

d Stop for crossing purposes only.

Great North of Scotland Railway Company.

THIRD
SUPPLEMENT TO WEEKLY CIRCULAR—No. 2320.

PASSENGER SUPERINTENDENT'S OFFICE,

ABERDEEN, 1st October, 1908.

SPECIAL ARRANGEMENTS :—

FRIDAY, 2nd October.

Fishworkers from Fraserburgh, Peterhead, Buckie, Cullen, Banff, &c., to Yarmouth and Lowestoft; and Mr. Boaze's Party, Dundee to Cruden Bay.

FISHWORKERS FROM FRASERBURGH TO YARMOUTH AND LOWESTOFT.

Down Special Trains.

(Empty Plant)	A.M.	A.M.		Up Special Trains. (Passengers.)	A.M.	P.M.	P.M.
Kittybrewster, dep.	9 50			Fraserburgh, dep.	5 40	6 5	6 5
Dyce	10 5			Lonmay			5 d17
Newmachar		10 44		Strichen			
Eddy		11 3		Maud	6 d5		
Ellon		11 20		Newmachar	6 22	6·50	6·50
Maud	10 40			Dyce	7·17	7·34	7·34
Dyce	11 15	12 d5		Aberdeen, arr.	7 33	7·42	7 42
Fraserburgh arr.	12 0	12 50				7·57	7 57

* Passing time   d Stops for crossing purposes only

5·40 p.m. Up Special Train will be too long for the Crossing Loop at Strichen, and it must be kept at Home Signal until 5·50 p.m. Down Train has arrived.

9·50 a.m. Down Special Train crosses 8·15 a.m and 9·30 a.m Up Trains at Ellon. It is to take 13 Carriages and 6 Vans East Coast plant from Kittybrewster to Fraserburgh.

10·30 a.m Down Special Train crosses 9·30 a.m Up Train at Newmachar, 8·15 a.m Up Goods Train at Udny, and 12·55 p.m Up Train at Fraserburgh. It is to take 4 Carriages and 2 Vans West Coast, and 3 Carriages and 1 Van Midland plant from Kittybrewster to Fraserburgh.

(Continued on page 277

Friday, 2nd October—continued.

FISHWORKERS FROM FRASERBURGH, &c.—continued

5·40 p.m Up Special Train crosses 5·50 p.m Down Train at Strichen and 7·0 p.m. Down Train at Dyce. It is to take Fishworkers and Luggage from Fraserburgh to Aberdeen *en route* for Yarmouth and Lowestoft, *via* East Coast.

6·5 p.m. Up Special Train crosses 5·50 p.m Down Train at Lonmay and 7·0 p.m. Down Train at Newmachar. It is to take Fishworkers and Luggage from Fraserburgh to Aberdeen *en route* for Yarmouth and Lowestoft, *via* West Coast and *via* Midland.

J. BAIN to be Guard of 9·50 a.m Down and 5·40 p.m Up Special Trains.

W. SMITH to be Guard of 10·30 a.m. Down and 6·5 p.m. Up Special Train

FISHWORKERS FROM PETERHEAD TO YARMOUTH AND LOWESTOFT.

Down Special Train. (Empty Plant)	A.M.		Up Special Train. (Passengers.)	P.M.
Kittybrewster, depart			Peterhead, depart	6 30
Dyce	11 10		Maud	*6·56
Newmachar	11 24		Udny	*7·41
Ellon	*11 40		Dyce	7·55
Maud	*11 57		Aberdeen, arrive	8 12
Peterhead, arrive	12·30			
	12 35			

* Passing time   d Stops for crossing purposes only

11·10 a.m Down Special Train crosses 9·30 a.m Up Train at Dyce, 8·15 a·m Up Goods Train at Newmachar 11·50 a.m. Up Goods Train (delayed) at Ellon, and 15 p·m Up Train at Peterhead. It is to take 6 Carriages and 3 Vans East Coast and 1 Carriage and 1 Van West Coast plant from Kittybrewster to Peterhead.

6·30 p.m Up Special Train crosses 4·27 p.m. Down Train at Peterhead and 7·0 p·m Down Train at Udny. It is to take Fishworkers and Luggage from Peterhead to Aberdeen *en route* for Yarmouth and Lowestoft—6 Carriages and 3 Vans by East Coast, and 1 Carriage and 1 Van by West Coast.

H. GRANT to be Guard.

FISHWORKERS FROM STATIONS PORTGORDON TO CULLEN INCLUSIVE AND BANFF.

Train. P.M.	Extra Vehicles.	From	To	
3·30	5 Thirds	Elgin	Aberdeen	Passengers to change at Aberdeen.
				Passengers and ordinary Coast portion from Grange. To call at most Stations.
12·55 (Goods) Dn.	2 Vans 1 Van	Buckie do.	Yarmouth for Luggage. Lowestoft	do.

Second Highland portion from Keith, and 6 Carriages and 3 Vans with Fishworkers and luggage from Grange. Train to be gone over at Grange, and to call only where required to set down Passengers.

Light Engine to leave Aberdeen at 8·15 p.m. and arrive Keith at 9·45 p.m.

5·33 p.m. Train will be run in two portions from Keith to Aberdeen, as follows:—

First.—K. and E. portion from Keith and ordinary Coast portion from Grange.

BRAKESMAN of 5·33 p.m Train to be Guard of First Portion
of 5·33 p.m Train to work alone

BRAKESMAN of 5·33 p.m Train to be Guard of Second Portion GUARD

BRAKESMAN of 12·55 p.m Coast Goods Train to be Guard of 5·15 p.m Train from Keith to Grange

THE BUCHAN SECTION
by
G. H. Robin

Like many other Scottish railway enthusiasts not resident in the Aberdeen or Elgin areas, the territory served by the old Great North of Scotland Railway never seemed to come within the scope of any journey I was required to make in my native country. Indeed, it was not until I had seen a representative of each of the pre-grouping English companies on its parent line that I was fated to come into contact with the old 'Great North', as it is still referred to up here.

In September 1944, I was transferred with dramatic suddenness from Portsmouth to a small village midway between Peterhead and Fraserburgh. Not only was it a great distance to move, but it was also a vast change in density of population and frequency of rail services. Gone now was the half-hourly service of multiple electric units, and in its place came three trains per day in each direction connecting this area with the town of Aberdeen, augmented by a varying number of goods and fast fish trains according to the season. The working of these trains was shared by rebuilt 'B12s' and some 'done' 4-4-0s of the parent line. Two return workings were restored in 1945 or 1946, thus making five services in each direction.

The Buchan trains, as the combined Peterhead and Fraserburgh trains are known, each consisted of a portion for either town and were divided at Maud Junction, 31 miles north of Aberdeen. Each portion had three vehicles — one third class coach, a first and third composite and then a passenger brake van. Most of them were of ex-Great Eastern origin, and while corridors were supplied on most sets, connecting gangways were not provided. Each set weighed only 72-80 tons tare according to stock. As the train engine always worked to Peterhead, the 'Blue Toon' portion was always marshalled in front on the down trains.

A 'B12' was usually in charge, and made quite a leisurely journey as far as Maud, whether on time or not. The 1 in 72 gradient up to Kittybrewster usually produced a speed of only 20-22½ m.p.h. Leaving the main line at Dyce Junction (6.2 miles), the branch immediately becomes single, and drops sharply for about ½ mile at 1 in 85 to cross the River Don near Parkhill Platform before commencing the 5 mile climb to the summit just beyond mile post 12¼. The bank starts off with 1½ miles at 1 in 105, followed by 1½ at 1 in 80 and finishing with 2 miles at 1 in 75. Newmachar Station, 11½ miles from Aberdeen, is ¾ of a mile short of the summit, so all down trains have to restart on the 1 in 75.

Trains, whether or not stopping at Parkhill, usually exceed 45 m.p.h. over the Don Bridge, but the 4 miles, or so, up to Newmachar, invariably reduced the speed to slightly under 30 m.p.h. in the case of the largest locomotives, and to 21 or 22 m.p.h. in the case of the 4-4-0s.

Dyce Station, with the main line seen on the left, and the Buchan Line, on the right.

G.N.S.R.A. Collection

Ellon Junction Station, photographed from the south, on 4th September 1955.

G.N.S.R.A. Collection

Maud Junction Station, with a North British diesel-electric locomotive, complete with snowploughs and token catcher, producing a flurry of exhaust.

C. Gammell

However, while time is often lost on the uphill stretches, the highest possible maximum speed is usually attempted between stations of the down stretches. The 2½ miles down at 1 in 80 from Newmachar to Udny, can be depended on to increase the speed from about 24 m.p.h. to between 55 and 60 m.p.h., although the 50 mark is hardly probable, although not unknown, on the shorter approaches to Logierieve, Esslemont and Ellon. With the exception of Parkhill, Logierieve and Esslemont, all are tablet stations.

Ellon used to be the junction for Cruden Bay and Boddam, to which section I will refer later, and it is situated ½ a mile from the foot of a 2 mile bank at 1 in 75 from crossing the River Ythan at the 19th mile post to the summit of the next watershed. Speed can be expected to rise to little over 25 m.p.h. at the latter point and over 50 m.p.h. will be attained on the gentle fall into Arnage, unless speed is checked owing to the distant being 'on', if a crossing is to be effected at this station.

From here to Auchnagatt (3.7 miles), the ruling grade is only 1 in 150, on which speed may rise to about 36 m.p.h., increasing to an average of 39 m.p.h. on the short 1 in 360 stretch. Thence the first 2¾ miles of the 4.1 miles to Maud Junction is against the engine at 1 in 200 steepening to 1 in 120, so the scheduled eight minutes are usually taken to the stop for dividing outside Maud Station. Here, 25-30 seconds is sufficient to detach the rear portion and allow the Peterhead coaches to draw forward and stop at the station in another 70 seconds or so. Maud Station has a 'V' platform, the western face taking both 'Up' and 'Down' Fraserburgh trains while the eastern face accommodates the 'Down' Peterhead trains. A separate platform is provided for trains from Peterhead.

From Maud to Peterhead, the line could be said to be gradually falling for the 13.2 miles, except for an aggregate of approximately 2 miles up at 1 in 100 and less, and over 60m.p.h. is often attained approaching Mintlaw and Longside Stations. If a train is running late, four minutes can be economised on this section.

Peterhead Station has an island platform, the northern face of which stops short at the station buildings, while the other continues to be completely covered in, thence to the buffers. A spur went round to the north of the station and engine shed, crossed the main Fraserburgh road on the level and continued for about ½ a mile down to the harbour. This section latterly fell into disuse and last year (1947) I noticed the rails had been lifted and some much needed repairs had been effected on the roadway at the level crossing.

The Maud–Fraserburgh section (16.0) miles is vastly different physically from the section just described. Two steep 'gables' have to be surmounted with stretches at 1 in 70, 1 in 75 and 1 in 60.

Leaving Maud, now possibly with an ex-GNSR 4-4-0, and about 72 to 80 tons, the 1.9 miles to Brucklay is up at 1 in 200 steepening to 1 in 70, but finishing with ¼ mile down at 1 in 80, and a few seconds can be economised on the five minutes allowed. Immediately on leaving this station, we start climbing right to the summit of the first 'gable', finishing off with 1½ miles at 1 in 75 to the summit between mile posts 34½ and 34¾. Once past the latter, we have 2 miles down, mostly at 1 in 60 to crossing the North Ugie River at Strichen. Furious battering seems to be the order of the day, and usually I get 30m.p.h. or slightly more at the top, but owing to the slack of 40m.p.h. over a curve approaching Strichen, the maximum speed is usually about 56m.p.h., although I have noted 60m.p.h. more than once.

From Strichen which, like Brucklay, is a crossing place, the grades alongside Mormond Hill to the next summit, at Mormond Halt, 2.3 miles further on, are easier, but once past the halt there are 2.6 miles down (0.6 mile at 1 in 80 and 2 miles at 1 in 70) to Lonmay, and the mile-a-minute rate is usually exceeded here. Lonmay, a typically GNSR wayside stone station, is the last block post before Fraserburgh. From Lonmay to Rathen the grades are gentle and in favour of the 'Down' trains, followed by a brief 1 in 80 facing 'Up' trains, before a level 2¼ miles past Philorth Halt and into the terminus.

Fraserburgh has two island platforms of fair length, but the outer face of the westernmost takes the lines leading to the engine sheds and the outer face and the other accommodates the St. Combs trains. A very large yard is provided, in view of the enormous fish traffic concentrated at this town, and in the height of the season a special engine is provided as yard shunter. It is a Kittybrewster engine and works north first thing in the morning and returns as pilot to the last fish train in the evening.

Before 'D40' 4-4-0, No. 6854 Southesk was withdrawn, I made several journeys to Aberdeen behind her on the 9.10a.m., which is described in the working timetables as 'EP' and she, sometimes relieved by another 4-4-0, made heavy weather of the 1 in 75 out of Lonmay. Speed often rose to 28 or

Fraserburgh Station, August 1953.

C. P. Knight

BR Standard 2-6-4T, No. 80005, waits at Fraserburgh with the 3.0 p.m. to Aberdeen on 11th September 1954.

W. A. Smith

29 m.p.h. before the 1 in 80; but if any fish vans were added, 23 or 24 m.p.h. would be about the maximum.

As the 1 in 60 out of Strichen is preceded by about ½ a mile of downhill track, speed usually fell a little on this bank (30 to 28 or 27 to 24 m.p.h according to the 'rush' made) while the speeds over 55 m.p.h. could be relied upon approaching both Strichen and Brucklay.

From Maud, the locomotive from the Peterhead section takes over all passenger trains with the exception of the train in question. There is nothing of note until Ellon is left, when 'Up' trains are faced with almost 7 miles, up to mile post 12½, made up roughly as follows: ¼ mile down at 1 in 75 to crossing the Ythan, then 1.3 miles to Esslemont followed by 1.5 mostly at 1 in 100 to Logierieve which is situated in the middle of a ¼ mile level stretch. By the time Udny is reached (1.8 miles), we are right on the 1 in 75 which continues to the summit. A long dreary stretch this is, with speeds of anything from 22 to 28 m.p.h. at the top, while a 'thirty' is a rarity, even with the 4-6-0 engines.

Down the four miles from Newmachar to Parkhill, good speeds are often attained and I have clocked 68 and 69 m.p.h. on several occasions.

'B12' 4-6-0s worked most of the trains throughout, between Aberdeen and Peterhead, although a 'D41' or 'D42' 4-4-0 used to take the 8.40 a.m. 'Down' train regularly. With the exception of the through working of the engine of the 9.10 a.m. from Fraserburgh, all passenger engines from this shed work on a shuttle principle to Maud and back.

In 1944, the daily goods still ran right through from Kittybrewster to Ellon, Cruden Bay and Boddam. However, in 1945 the branch started to fill up with wagons awaiting repair, until in 1946 its entire length (except, of course, for occupation sidings) of 15.6 miles, was occupied but for a short length at Ellon which was used as a shunting neck. By this time, (1948), the line had been cleared to about Hatton Station.

It would not be right to leave the Buchan section without a few words on the St. Combs Light Railway. This line, 5.1 miles long, runs for 0.8 mile alongside the main Aberdeen line (giving the appearance of a double track) before turning through the local golf course. It then followed the contour of the land with grades of 1 in 50. Inverallochy, with its single platform, is the only intermediate station. Twenty minutes are allowed in either direction. St. Combs terminus merely consists of a single platform, a run-round loop and a small yard.

Ex-GER 'F4' 2-4-2 tank, No. 7222 (later 7164) is at Fraserburgh for working the branch, and two ex-GNSR 4-4-0s, one passenger and one goods, are normally stabled here as well. No. 2277 *Gordon Highlander* was the passenger engine in 1947, but No. 62231 has since replaced it.

In the summer of 1948, brightly painted and clean 'B1s' handled the bulk of the fish traffic while the odd passenger had to be content with his dingy black four-coupled steed; although for my part, and for any enthusiast, I would say, it is a tonic to find a pre-grouping engine in its own rural surroundings.

The above article is reproduced with permission of the author and is based on an article by him which appeared in the *Stephenson Locomotive Society Journal* in 1948.

Fraserburgh 1898 — a view, looking south, from Dalrymple Hall Tower showing the links and part of the station yard, before the building of the St. Combs branch and the enlargement of the station. This was also before the construction of the Consolidated Pneumatic Tool Works.

F. Tocher Collection

THE WEST BUCHAN LIGHT RAILWAY

The Light Railway Act of 1896 resulted in a considerable number of proposals to open up rural Britain, by way of a network of lines constructed to meet the minimum requirements set by this statute.

In the north-east of Scotland, several schemes were discussed, but only one line was built, the one from Fraserburgh to St. Combs.

An interesting proposition was the building of a narrow gauge railway line from Maud to Turriff serving the communities of Cuminestown, Garmond, New Byth and New Pitsligo. This project was favoured both before and after the First World War but, inevitably, the increase in motor transport in the early 1920s killed the idea.

A group known as the 'Scottish Light Railways and Development Syndicate' conducted much research in the matter and its plans make interesting reading.

Originally, the track gauge was to be 2ft. 6in., but later proposals increased this to 3ft. A considerable body of opinion felt, however, that a standard gauge link would be far more sensible as transhipment would be avoided.

Local landlords were sympathetic as was the GNSR which was reportedly quite willing to work the line providing suitable arrangements were agreed. The railway which would have been 21 miles 4 furlongs in length had been intended to benefit the largely agricultural community in the area and traffic would have been almost exclusively agricultural in nature. It was estimated that 27,500 tons of goods would be carried yearly with about 1,500 tons of this being coal. Some peat and stone traffic would originate at New Pitsligo. Passenger traffic, to be catered for in tramway-type coaches, would amount to 20,000 journeys per annum, and there would also be some livestock conveyed. It was said that the parishes to be served by the line had a population of 27,000, the largest being the community of New Pitsligo.

Facilities would have been sparse with no buildings apart from wooden sheds at seven points. I have no information as to whether the main depot would have been at Turriff or at Maud.

It appears that the railway would have followed the public road out of Turriff for some distance before cutting across the undulating agricultural land to New Pitsligo, where it would have run down the centre of the High Street. It was then to follow the side of the main road to about Brucklay. Due to the nature of the countryside and the cheapness of the construction, the ruling gradient would be 1 in 45.

The line was favoured not only for its local nature, but as a short route for passengers from Banff to Fraserburgh. I do not feel that there would have been much through freight traffic because of the need for transhipment!

The line would have been steam worked, although the possibility of electric traction was investigated. The promoters had been interested by the apparent success of the Aberdeen Suburban Tramways, and some rural electric lines in England and Ireland. On the same basis, they foresaw, apparently, no difficulty in street running!

An application was made for a Treasury Grant, and negotiations with the Board of Agriculture for Scotland and with the Light Railway Commissioners were far advanced when the outbreak of war in 1914 caused the scheme to be shelved. After the war, it was again proposed but, by this time, road transport was developing quickly and the project was never proceeded with.

Had it been built, the line would inevitably have met with an early closure, but the prospect of a narrow gauge railway meandering through Buchan is a pleasing thought.

TICKET STORIES
one of an occasional series
by
J. L. McAllan

Away back in 1910, R. T. M., a small farmer from the Lonmay district, had been on honeymoon in Aberdeen with his bride, wee Beanie. When they entered the 'Joint' Station, to make for home on the 7.00p.m. Buchan train, R. T. M. discovered, to his horror, that he had lost one of the return halves of the tickets. As they were approaching the booking office, Beanie spotted something on the ground and picked it up. Here was a 1st class single to Maud, which some unfortunate gent had presumably dropped earlier in the day! This would at least take them to Maud, and so they joined the rear portion of the 7.00p.m. on platform 11. In the non-corridor compartment they were joined by two other Lonmay 'billies' — Lang Tom Burr and Wee Willie Horner, on their way back from the mart. The ticket inspector, making his customary check before the departure, looked with some suspicion at the two tickets offered by R. T. M., as a 3rd return half to Lonmay and a 1st single to Maud seemed strange bedfellows; but on the face of it, both were in order, and he said nothing.

At the head of the train was Manson 4-4-0, No. 72. The Peterhead-based driver was a well-known character whose name is now forgotten but whose impatient and aggressive manner had earned him the nickname of 'The Tiger'. The weather had been stormy all day and 'The Tiger' was anxious to get home without delay.

At Dyce, the Lonmay company was joined by Lizzie Buchan, a Fraserburgh fishwife, who had been peddling her wares in Inverurie and had changed out of the 5.50p.m. ex-Insch. A rather elegant spoken Englishman also joined, after enquiring whether a seat was available, (but without getting an answer). He alighted at Ellon, with a polite 'Goodnight, ladies and gentlemen'. 'At's a gabbin vratch!' commented Lang Tom Burr.

At Arnage, the train was booked to cross the 7.05p.m. ex-Peterhead/ 7.00p.m. ex-Fraserburgh, but when 'The Tiger' drew up there, on time at 8.05p.m., he noted that the other train had not arrived and the 'up' home signal was still 'on'. As his fireman was handing the tablet to the young signalman — in his first box in sole charge — 'The Tiger' said, 'Is 'at b--- nae comin' yet?'. 'I suppose he'll be held up wi' the sna',' replied the signalman. 'Sna!' snapped 'The Tiger', 'Fat dis he ken aboot sna; he's jist a toonser'. (A most unfair remark, since every driver on the Buchan had all day been struggling against the weather). 'Onywey, a'm nae bidin' here; lat me on tae Auchnagatt'. The signalman stood there, torn between fear of the driver and fear of deviating from the booked routine. 'Let's see a haud o yer shovel, Andy,' said the driver, 'and a'll sort 'im'. 'The Tiger' plunged the shovel into

The staff at Ellon Junction Station.

G.N.S.R.A. Collection

Ellon Junction Station (circa 1910) with the arrival of the Peterhead and Fraserburgh train.

G.N.S.R.A. Collection

the firebox and drew out a full load of red-hot cinders, which he menacingly pointed at the signalman. That was enough. The train was immediately offered to Auchnagatt, and, as the 'up' train had not been heard of there from Maud, was accepted. At Auchnagatt, the 'up' train had still not arrived, nor indeed had the 6.30p.m. goods from Fraserburgh, which should have crossed the 'down' train there. So 'The Tiger' was given the road through to Maud.

The usual stop was made at the south end of Maud, and after detaching the Fraserburgh portion, 'The Tiger' took his train into the Peterhead 'down' platform. The 7.05p.m. passenger ex-Peterhead was in the 'up' platform, waiting for its Fraserburgh portion which was nowhere to be seen. This meant that the 'down' Fraserburgh portion lacked a locomotive. Obviously something had gone wrong on the Fraserburgh branch. Happily, 'The Tiger' was allowed to proceed to Peterhead!

On arrival at the Broch, the driver of the 4.38p.m. ex-Aberdeen had reported that the line between Strichen and Lonmay was 'fillin up gey quick'. There was a snowplough engine at Fraserburgh, and it was decided to send it south in advance of the 7.00p.m. passenger. Additionally it was decided, in order to minimise passenger delay, to run the 6.30p.m. goods after the passenger.

The snowplough engine duly reached Maud about twenty minutes after the 'down' passenger, and sped on south to Kittybrewster. Ten minutes later, the Fraserburgh 'up' passenger at last arrived. The two 'up' trains were quickly united and went forward. Then the Broch branch engine, another Manson 4-4-0, turned and took the 'down' coaches into the station. It had been hoped that the 6.30p.m. goods would, by this time, have been into the goods loop adjoining the Fraserburgh platform road, but when the signalman tried to 'set the road' for it, it was found that snow had jammed the loop points at the north end. Thus faced with more delay, many of the passengers for the Fraserburgh branch, including the bridal couple, Tam and Williw and Lizzie Buchan, decided to get some heat in the station buffet. Good use was made of this half-hour break by all — even by Lizzie Buchan despite the teetotal protestations which she had voiced on the train.

At last, about 9.15p.m. they got on their way. Clearly the weather was getting worse, but the passengers were nevertheless in good fettle with the Maud spirit and the prospect of getting home soon. As the train raced downhill through blin'drift, wee Beanie saw light appearing dimly. 'Far's this?' she asked. 'Michty, div ye nae ken Strichen?', said her man. 'Oh Strichen!' said she, and she burst into song:

'There's as good fish into the sea,
As ever yet was taken,
I'll cast my line and try again,
I'm only since forsaken,
So I'll gae doon tae Strichen toon,
Where I was bred and born,
And there I'll get anither sweetheart,
Will mairry me the morn'.

'Ho, ho', said Wee Willie Horner, 'Div ye hear that, Robbie; she's lookin' for anither lad! Are ye striven already'? 'Eh Beanie'! Could ye be deein' wi' a bit kittle,' said Lang Tom, putting his brawny hand round her waist. At this, R. T. M.'s face took on a look that would have done justice to the go-ahead aspect of a guard's lamp. 'Jealous, are ye?' said Lizzie Buchan. Roused, R. T. M. snapped back, 'Ony mair lip fae you, Lizzie Buchan, an I'll pit ye in ower ye're ain creel an' bung ye oot into the sna'. (In view of Lizzie's ample girth, a most unlikely proposition, but, unknown to them all, the creel would soon enough have its uses).

With all this backchat, no one noticed the reduction in speed until the train came to a halt in Mormond cutting. There was a faint sound of voices outside, and a much less faint sound of the wind blowing snow against the windows. At length, the guard appeared and announced, 'Weel, fowks, I some doot we're founert. There's an awfa drift up there; she'll niver mak it the nicht. Ye'd better a' cam oot an traival ben to the station. The agent's got a gweed fire goin' in the waiting room'.

'A weel, I wis needin oot onywey', sighed Wee Willie Horner.

And so they all struggled through the snow to the Mormond waiting-room, their unity, if not their sobriety, restored. Lang Tom Burr escorted Lizzie Buchan through the worst of the drifts. R. T. M. took Lizzie's creel and actually managed to carry wee Beanie inside it. All the passengers spent the night and much of the following day at Mormond until relief came. Although Lonmay was only two miles away, there could be no question of any attempt to walk home through the blizzard.

With about twenty passengers all told, there was little chance of sleep, but they all had a fairly merry time, which they remembered with some relish for many years. One thing wee Beanie remembered in particular — never to sing 'Mormond Braes' in the presence of her husband.

But one thing was not remembered — the excess on the ticket from Maud to Lonmay.

January 1909 — the snow has filled the notorious cutting, known as Satan's Den, just north of Newmachar.

LONGSIDE BRANCH RAILWAY
by
John Emslie and Richard Jackson

On reading through the Association's booklet published for the 'Formartine and Buchan Excursion' on 24th May 1969, we were surprised that no mention had been made of the branch railway which existed at Longside from 1918 to 1923. In the mid-1950s, Mr Rigby, who was then District Civil Engineer, BR Aberdeen, and his assistant Mr Graham, unearthed, from their files, several plans pertaining to this branch. Although, in some respects, the information remains scanty, we think it is of interest and value now to place on record in the *Review* the details gleaned from these documents and other sources.

The 'Great North' apparently acted as agents for the construction of the line, and in May 1917, the Board wrote to the Admiralty giving the cost of the proposed railway as £19,042. *(See Note 1, Page 97)*. Three months later, the Railway Executive Committee asked for work to be put in hand, and the line was surveyed in October. It followed the route indicated on the map on *Page 95* which is based on the engineers' plans and ground evidence. The GNSR carried out any works required at Longside Station but the remainder of the construction for the branch was undertaken by Messrs. Tawse, (Contractors), Aberdeen whose tender of £23,015 13s 9d was accepted on behalf of the Admiralty in February 1918. *(See Note 1, Page 97)*. However, construction was slow to start because a letter dated 7th October 1918 referred to commencement 'as soon as possible'. Possibly part of the delay may have been due to the cancellation of the original proposal (Tawse plan dated 11th February 1918) for a single slip connection off the station loop lines at Longside. In fact, the Railway Executive Committee which controlled the disposition of rail facilities at that time, permitted installation of only a trailing crossover which linked the branch to the 'up' loop at Longside. *(See sketch of track layout at Longside)*.

On Monday, 28th October 1918, the east points of the loop at Longside had been shifted and were brought into use at their new location nearer Peterhead. Presumably, this heralded the start of work on the branch proper which curved southwards on an embankment to cross the South Ugie Water. This crossing was accomplished by means of a 60 ft. long, 3 span timber trestle on a skew alignment. From the river, another embankment carried the line on to rising ground as it approached the public road (the present A950), connecting Mintlaw and Peterhead. The road crossing was ungated but timber cattle guards were installed, as too were warning boards. These boards were of two types – the road warnings were lettered 'CAUTION, Railway Level Crossing, LOOK OUT FOR TRAINS' whereas the rail warnings indicated 'WHISTLE for road level crossing. SPEED NOT TO EXCEED 10 MILES PER HOUR'. Similar boards were provided at the other principal crossings on the

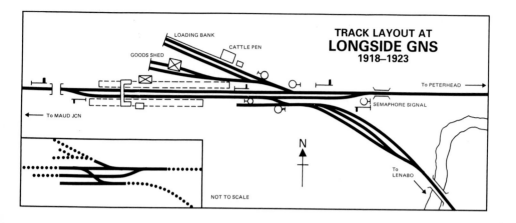

line but despite the warnings, at least one collision occurred between a train and a road vehicle. On 15th August 1923, a train and a motor car collided at the main road crossing just mentioned.

The branch continued southwards and westwards, apparently following the undulations of the land with only minimal earthworks. Several minor roads and watercourses were traversed before the line reached the perimeter fence of the airship station. The maximum gradient on the route was 1 in 60 with the majority of curves aligned at 20 chains radius. Only one curve on the actual 'main line' was less than this — 15 chains radius. Rails on the branch were in 36 ft. lengths set on 7 ft. x 10 ft. sleepers spaced at 2 ft. 9 in. centres. To assist with the location of the route, we have deduced the approximate National Grid Reference applicable to the main features of the branch. All are in square 'NK':

Longside Station (GNSR)	039478
Bridge over South Ugie Water	044476
Farm road	047472
Public roads:	
Tiffery—Kinmundy	045456
Stream	045455
Public roads:	
Ludquharn—Kinmundy	042447
Auchtydore—Peterhead	040435
Farm road	035433
Stream	033431
Farm road	029428
Junction	028428
Terminus:	
Main track	027429
Spur track	029427

The third sketch has been prepared from the Tawse plans deposited with the railway engineer at Guild Street and also from information gathered on the site of the airship station. It shows the layout of the airship station and the trackwork both proposed and, as probably constructed.

These run-round loops were provided, although one of these was only partly within the naval perimeter. One loop was adjacent to a petrol store (tank wagon supplies or barrels/cans in open wagons or vans), and another served the electricity powerhouse. Originally, the latter was intended to serve a coke store by means of a right angle junction utilizing a wagon turntable, but seemingly, this did not materialize. The purpose of the spur track with the third loop is not clear but may have been for the delivery of airship parts.

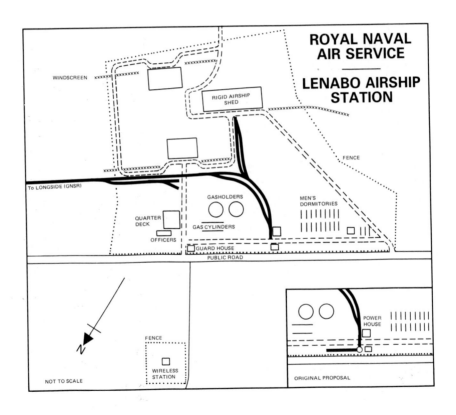

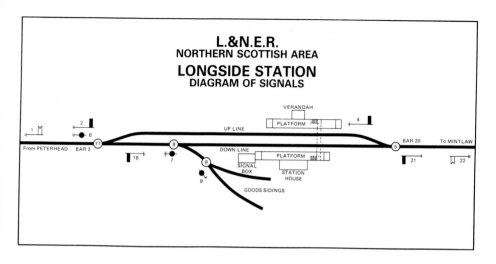

Very little information exists as to the operation of this branch and it would be most interesting and illuminating if any naval personnel of that time could be traced and their recollections placed on record. Sir Malcolm Barclay-Harvey's book states that the GNSR Beyer Peacock 0-4-0 well tank engines were sold in 1916 to the Admiralty to work this line. This does not seem to tally with the absence of construction work suggested by the minutes and plans dated 1917 and the letter of 7th October 1918 already mentioned. It has also been suggested that a fireless engine worked the line but as there was apparently no provision for stabling or servicing an engine, was one ever allocated to Lenabo, or did a 'Great North' engine work the branch? E. A. Pratt *(See Note 2)*, records that 31,913 tons of traffic was worked over the line during its relatively short life which ended in 1923 when the trackwork, south from the main line (GNS) connection, was removed on 7th September according to a note entered on the District Civil Engineer's plan.

After a lapse of almost 50 years, it is surprising how much still remains of this lightly constructed line. The embankment from Longside Station exists to a point just south of the river. After a gap of about ½ mile to the crossing of the main Peterhead road, a shallow cutting is clearly visible for about a quarter of a mile alongside a farm road. The next three-quarters of a mile to Nether Kinmundy has virtually disappeared, but from there, on the formation, is almost complete to its terminus inside the Forestry Commission woods at Lenabo. In fact not only the railway but much of the airship station itself is still clearly discernible among the trees.

Notes:

1. *GNSR Minute Book*
2. *British Railways and the Great War* – Selwyn Blount Ltd.
   London, 1921

TICKET STORIES
one of an occasional series
by
A. W. Coutts

Maybe the milk had been off; maybe the eggs for breakfast were bad, but more likely it was that last 'wee dram' he had been bought by Archie Duguid that sent him reeling queasily around the room at the cold grey hour of four. Even more likely, thought A.F.C., it was the other 'wee drams' he had been bought at the 'Royal' the night before which were sending his stomach into uncontrollable spasms at four on a Saturday morning. His face ashen, his eyes bloodshot, his temples pounding, A.F.C. packed his 'trunk' and half walking, half crawling, wound his way down stairs, out into the close and along the street towards the station.

LNER Class 'D40', No. 62275 *Sir David Stewart* (ex-GNSR No. 47) awaits departure from Peterhead with a passenger train in 1952.

N. R. Knight

By 7.15, and the departure of his train, A.F.C. had regained his composure enough to contemplate the dewy landscape spread out before him. The locomotive at the head of the train, *Kinmundy*, newly out of the works at Kittybrewster, had obviously never heard of A.F.C.'s condition or, indeed, if it had, it would never have insisted on first whistling and secondly applying its brakes with such a cacophonous cascade that even the skies seem to shake.

Maud was reached, and there the Fraserburgh portion was attached, the locomotive, No. 4, a 4-4-0, built by Kitson, resplendent in its newly shopped livery. Maud was, indeed, a hive of activity with the two locomotives engaged in shunting operations and the platforms piled high with parcels, crates, boxes and miscellenaneous livestock, all adding to the seeming confusion. As if by magic, the scene was changed before A.F.C.'s still bleary bloodshot eyes. The 'cargo' was hustled aboard, the engines coupled together and away went the train. Auchnagatt, Arnage and Ellon were reached and passed, the train moving at speed across the landscape as it headed towards Aberdeen.

By the time Dyce was reached, the sun shone brightly out of a clear, if icy, blue sky and A.F.C. was back at his spritely best, the clean air having removed the last embers of firewater from his brain. At Dyce, the carriage sheds were resounding as the 'tankies' proceeded to shunt the carriages for the 'subbies'. Altogether there were three tanks in the sidings; Nos. 11 and 39 of Manson's 0-6-0 Class 'D' and one of the later Class 'E' 0-6-0s, No. 37. Perhaps it was only right, thought A.F.C., that these diminutive, indeed inconspicuous looking, locomotives should have charge of the shunting operations for it seemed as though he was gazing upon some tiny model spread before him. His window was the viewpiece by which he surveyed the changing scene, as though it was his empire.

At last, at 9.20a.m., the 'Joint' was reached and, after adjusting his apparel suitably, A.F.C, grabbing his trunk up in his broad arms, made his way towards the southern end of the station in time to see a 'CR' 4-4-0, No. 124, *Eglinton*, appear from the general direction of the Ferryhill engine sheds, beautifully resplendent in its blue livery. With increasing interest A.F.C. put his trunk on the 'barra' and settled down to watch the multifarious collection of engines which were to be seen shunting in the yards. Altogether A.F.C. counted six engines at the south end — three belonging to the 'Caley', two to the 'NB' and a foreigner dressed somberly in black, although, to this day, no person knows from whence it came.

By 9.45a.m. and the departure of his train, A.F.C. had become quite intrigued with the workings of the railway and was settled down for a comfortable journey. The calm of the morning was, however, proving a direct contrast to the hustle and bustle of the previous night. By Cove Bay, his eyes were weary; by Portlethen his mind was blank; by Newtonhill his body was tired and by Stonehaven he was asleep.

Alas, all good things come to an end and this was no exception. With an ear-splitting heart-rendering screech, the brakes were applied shaking A.F.C. like a puppet suspended on a string. Picking himself up from his dusty seat (having landed with a thud on the floor) his head was soon seen protruding from the window of the compartment, each muscley sinew bulging and straining at the effort of peering through the steam being blown off by No. 124 as it stood by Laurencekirk's home signal. 'Typical', thought A.F.C., 'not even the 'Great North' would be so unthinking as to actually wake someone up on account of a mere signal'.

The delay, however, was not to prove series and in a matter of moments the signal was down and the train was away, although this feat was not always performed in that order. Marykirk was reached and passed as was the fate of Craigo before Dubton was reached and A.F.C. found himself compelled to leave, aided by the gentle hand of the guard. Crossing the platform, A.F.C. boarded the two coach train standing in the loop platform and, with the 0-4-4 tank newly built that year at St. Rollox blowing off steam at the head of the train, it was not long before the train was away along the branch to Montrose (CR).

At Montrose and journey's end, A.F.C. had just time to reflect on the tribulations of travel and the acquisition of a momento (his ticket), before scurrying away in a cloud of dust and out into the midday sun. The reason — why, to find a bed for the night, of course!!

ACCIDENT AT BRUCKLAY — 1889

During the 1880s, the financial position of the GNSR was poor for various reasons. Improvement of the permanent way and operating methods, therefore, was slow and often the result of experience. As a result, several accidents occurred during the decade.

One such took place at Brucklay on 25th July 1889 and illustrates the rather backward way of the time. The 2.40 p.m. train to Aberdeen, hauled by a 4-4-0, driven by John Reiach, with John Park as fireman, consisted of seven vans. It had left Fraserburgh a few minutes late and approached Brucklay downhill at about 25 m.p.h. It was not booked to stop there but as he entered the station the driver sensed something was amiss. The train had been diverted into the middle goods siding!

Reiach applied both his Westinghouse brake and the steam reverser, but was too late to prevent the engine crashing into a row of wagons parked there. These disintegrated on impact. By a cruel stroke of luck, an elderly crofter, George Fowlie, a man from the New Pitsligo area, was unloading wood from one of these trucks. On impact, he was killed instantly and his body was thrown some distance, eventually to be found underneath an overturned coach.

The engine itself was derailed, its front end being buried in the wreckage of the wagons. Its chimney was knocked off and its front bogie was split. The coaches were also extensively damaged but, fortunately, neither the train crew, nor most of the 30 to 40 passengers were hurt. A train was sent from Maud to collect them and. later in the afternoon, a breakdown crane left

Brucklay Station, 25th January 1964.

C. Gammell

Kittybrewster for the scene of the accident; several of the GNSR top officials travelled with it.

Naturally, in view of the fatality, a Board of Trade accident enquiry ensued. This was conducted by Colonel Rich and proved very critical of the Railway Company's operation.

Several surprising facts emerged. The points and signals at Brucklay were not at that time interlocked. The main line distant signal, 293 yards north of the station, showed all clear, but the 12ft. high indicator at the points was at danger! In addition, the pointsman, as was the custom at Brucklay at the time, was waving the train through the station with a white flag! The pointsman, a youth named Tocher, who had been with the Company only 23 days, understandably fainted when he saw the accident.

Colonel Rich criticised this practice as it distracted the driver's attention. He also pointed out that Tocher had been on duty for 10 hours and the driver for 7. It was wrong for the GNSR to employ such a young and inexperienced man in such a responsible position and all the blame was not laid on him.

Thus the GNSR was severely censured for outmoded and provedly dangerous operating techniques.

THE CIRCUS COMES TO TOWN

Readers of the February 1965 *Review* may recollect an article on the visit of Buffalo Bill and his Wild West Show to Peterhead and Fraserburgh. In August 1954 Bertram Mills Circus visited Aberdeen, Fraserburgh, Huntly and Elgin.

This entailed a number of heavy special trains over the 'Great North'. The last performance of the circus in Aberdeen was on Saturday evening, 15th August at the Bridge of Don. Preparations had started early on that morning at Kittybrewster where three 'specials' were marshalled. Before the last act had left the ring, equipment was on the move and by 10.30 p.m., train No. 600 was on the move to Fraserburgh. It was followed by No. 601 at 2.00 a.m. (16th) and the last left at 8.00 a.m. The signal boxes on the line were open all night to pass the trains and the returning light engines. Fraserburgh box remained open all day Sunday. The locomotives of No. 600 worked, on their return to Kittybrewster, some of the stock to Maud for storage.

Train No.	Locomotives	Vehicles	Load
600	61347/50	24	620 tons
601	61349/52	22	635 tons
602	61242	17	250 tons

All the vehicles were checked and, where necessary, repaired for the trip to Huntly on the Thursday (20th). There was only a matinee performance on that day at Fraserburgh and the specials went to Dyce where the locomotives were to be changed and the fitted stock remarshalled:

Train No.	Fraserburgh Depart	Locos to Dyce	Locos ex-Dyce
600	9.00 p.m.	61307/46	61502/90041
601	12.30 a.m.	61347/51	61779/90455
602	7.15 a.m.	61350	61350

The engine change for No. 602 had to be cancelled as Kittybrewster had scraped the bottom of the barrel for power.

At Huntly, Nos. 600 and 601 could not be run round to shunt them into the yard, the connection to which trails in on the 'up' side; the crossovers were too close together. These trains were turned on the Grange triangle, a 'B1' from Keith being used to haul them from Grange Junction to Grange North Junction. The train engine had the token for the Grange–Grange North section while the 'B1' had the token for the Grange North–Glenbarry section. On the return, the trains were shunted into the yard at Huntly.

We are indebted to Dr J. Emslie for the information which was incorporated in an article in *Trains Illustrated*, October 1954.

ARNAGE – 12TH MARCH 1874
by
R. P. Jackson

The first head-on collision on a single line section of the GNSR occurred about 3.00p.m. on 12th March 1874, when a light engine collided with the 1.20p.m. mixed train to Peterhead near Arnage. With the operating methods then in force, it is a wonder that there had not been trouble long before, and it is true to say that the Company owed more than it realised to the discipline of its footplate staff.

As often happens, the events leading up to the accident can be traced back quite a long way, in this case to a severe snow storm two days earlier. Among other troubles, this blocked the Buchan line and also led to driver John MacDonald and his fireman, Alex Scott, working some very long hours. Their normal turn involved the 1.30a.m. 'down' main line goods, returning from Keith on a similar train at 6.50a.m. Due to the storm, when they returned to Aberdeen on the 10th, they were put out to assist the 11.50a.m. goods as far as Udny, which meant they did not book off until nearly 3.00p.m. The next day, they were again kept on duty to assist, if needed, on the Buchan line and were not released until about 4.00p.m.

Because of these two long days, they were rostered for a short duty on the 12th and should have worked a 'cattle special' to Logierieve, but it was cancelled owing to the snow. Instead, they were once again sent to assist the 11.50a.m., this time as far as Auchnagatt, its normal destination. On this occasion, however, it was extended to Peterhead, so MacDonald and his mate took over the train engine's return working, light to Ellon, followed by the 3.20p.m. 'up' goods from there. Usually, the guard would have returned with them, instead of which he worked through to Peterhead.

The train reached Auchnagatt about 20 minutes late at 2.46p.m. and after the pilot had uncoupled and moved on to the 'up' line, the guard, Gordon Paterson, realizing that MacDonald was a stranger, called to him 'We cross at Arnage normally, whether we do today or not'. In reply MacDonald just nodded, and shortly after he asked the stationmaster, James Barron, if there were any instructions for him, as would have been the case in any altered working, but there were none.

Barron, who had been at Auchnagatt for just over a year, also saw that MacDonald was a stranger but it never occurred to him to check that he knew the crossing at Arnage. In fact, one can detect an almost querulous note in his evidence at the subsequent inquiry. 'I gave him no instructions as to where he was to pass the other train, and I am not in the habit of giving instructions unless I receive them. I had not seen him at Auchnagatt since I had been at the station, but yet I did not think it necessary to ascertain whether he knew where he should cross the train from Aberdeen'.

Meanwhile, the 1.20p.m. 'down' mixed, also double-headed, was approaching Ellon. The leading engine, running chimney first, was driven by William Strachan and fired by John Kemp with a brakesman called Scott also on the footplate. The second engine, No. 5, was tender first with John Beat as driver and John Chalmers firing. The train itself consisted of 12 loaded waggons followed by a 3rd class brake in which rode another brakesman. Behind this came a 1st class carriage, a 3rd class carriage and finally a brakevan which carried the guard, Alexander Burnett. Because of late running, this train left Ellon at 2.42p.m., 18 minutes behind schedule.

The scene now shifts to Arnage where there were three men on duty. George Anderson had been stationmaster for rather over two years. With him were William Gordon, porter for the last 14 months and the booking clerk, William Bruce. The latter was 14 years old and had been working there for 8 months at a wage of 6/3d (31p) per week. At 2.50p.m., the light engine and the 'down' train were both signalled on the telegraph, with the train entry recorded first in the book.

By present day standards, the signalling arrangements were primitive. For each direction there was a home signal standing on, and worked from, the platform, while the corresponding distant signal was operated by a lever near the points at each end of the loop. The 'up' distant was 629 yards from its home signal.

A few minutes after the telegraph message, Anderson went to the north points and Gordon to the south ones, leaving Bruce to work the home signal. Presently the approaching light engine, which was travelling at about 15 m.p.h., whistled, and Anderson lowered the distant signal. Bruce then lowered the home signal to caution, which was the usual way of working. When the engine passed the distant signal, Anderson returned it to danger. On reaching the points, the driver applied steam which made the stationmaster realise the engine was not going to stop, so he shouted and waved, but to no avail.

Young Bruce, on the other hand, was not concerned to see the engine steaming, as he had often seen this done even by engines due to stop at the station. As it passed him he returned the signal to danger but made no attempt to stop the engine.

Meanwhile, down at the south points, William Gordon was alarmed when the engine passed his cabin. He rushed out waving his arms and then returned for his red flag and waved that. When he saw that these had no effect, he worked his distant signal up and down until the wire broke.

All this proved useless. The engine steamed on and the inevitable collision occurred at Gallowhill, about ¼ mile further on. The light engine broke away from its tender, which was badly damaged, and ran back about 50 yards down the gradient towards Arnage. Both the other engines were derailed along with their tenders and the first waggon of the train. The leading engine's smokebox was broken off and its tender destroyed. No. 5 suffered only superficial damage, but its tender was also beyond repair. The rest of the train remained on the rails and was undamaged.

Strachan, driving the leading engine, was killed at once. Kemp, his fireman, died the next day, while Scott was so severely injured that he was unable to give evidence at the inquiry some 5 weeks later. MacDonald succumbed to his injuries the following day. The remainder of the footplate staff jumped clear and were, more or less, unhurt. Among the passengers, four complained of injury.

Needless to say, the Company had to pay compensation. John Kemp's family got £105 while the families of both drivers were given £160. As for the passengers, Mr Armstrong asked for £100, but settled for half that sum. Mr Oserate began by demanding £200, refused an offer of £100 but eventually agreed to accept £75. Mr Thompson accepted £5 10s 0d (£5.50p), and Mr Whitehill £31 10s 0d (£31.50p). Mr & Mrs Davidson, who farmed Gallowhill, were given £75 for their 'attention and trouble', with which they were very satisfied.

A number of doctors seemed to have been involved in attending the injured. Dr Reid of Ellon was paid £52 10s 0d (£52.50p) for three months attention, and this did not include nursing or medicines. Dr Pirie, Aberdeen, said he would expect £12 12s 0d (£12.60p) and that Drs Fiddes and Hill who accompanied him would also expect fees. By this time the Board seem to have had enough so they offered Dr Pirie and Dr Fiddes £10 10s 0d (£10.50p) each, while Dr Hill would have to be content with half that amount. This he declined on the grounds that he should be paid the same as the others. History does not relate the end of this particular haggle.

The inquiry was held by Captain H. W. Tyler on 18th April. His report begins by quoting the arrangements for working single line traffic as given in the Company's Working Timetable. 'A single line across the column, thus —— denotes the stations appointed for the trains to meet and pass each other, and in no case shall a train passing in one direction leave the station where a train coming in the opposite direction has to pass, until the said train has first arrived and passed into the station clear of the points'. Any alteration to the printed arrangements had to be in writing, or by telegraph, from the Train & Traffic Superintendent, Mr Morrison. He goes on to say that under these rules the engines' drivers were themselves held responsible for obeying these instructions.

The timetable quite clearly showed, and repeated in the accompanying notes, that the light engine due to leave Auchnagatt at 2.35p.m., crossed the 1.20p.m. 'down' at Arnage.

Alexander Scott, the light engine's fireman, was the first witness. Although he had become MacDonald's fireman in the autumn of 1868, he was obviously still rather overawed by him. He heard him ask for instructions at Auchnagatt but did not hear what was said. In any case, MacDonald was not in the habit of passing on such information. He corroborated the evidence about the signals approaching Arnage but did not see the stationmaster waving. According to him, the porter was outside the cabin at the south points and this made him think there might be a train coming. At no time did he see this man waving even though he looked back at him. So as to be sure of his facts before speaking to the driver, he started to look at his timetable, but before he could refer to the proper place he saw the other train coming, shouted and jumped clear. He estimated that they were running at 25-30 m.p.h. when the collision occurred.

The bulk of the rest of the evidence was given by the staffs of the stations at Auchnagatt and Arnage, and the crews of the other train. It covered the events chronicled above, so it need not be repeated.

Because so much of this incident concerns MacDonald's actions, it is worth studying him in some detail. He joined the 'Great North' in January 1862 and, until 31st January 1866, was employed on shunting at Waterloo and working up to Kittybrewster. After 9 months on the Buchan line and 3 months with construction trains at Denburn, he was spare for six weeks. On 16th March 1867, he took up a regular goods turn on the main line, working the 3.40a.m. 'down' returning with the 11.15a.m. Finally, on 29th December 1869, he moved to the 1.30a.m. 'down' goods, returning from Keith with the goods, leaving there at 6.50a.m. He continued with occasional workings on the Buchan line and is credited with 36 trips, mainly assisting to Udny, between 27th January 1870 and 4th June 1873. Indeed, the last time he had been beyond Udny was on 31st October 1871, also on the 11.50a.m., but at that time it terminated at Arnage and crossed the northbound train at Ellon. He was stated to be one of the steadiest drivers in the Company's service, a strict teetotaller, strong willed and a man upon whom the greatest reliance could be placed. Prior to his death, he told both his wife and Mr Barnett, the Engineer, that he was convinced he had to cross the other train at Ellon, which we have seen was the case when he was last so far north, two years earlier.

Captain Tyler's report was critical. He accepted that MacDonald was entirely to blame, but added that if the driver had had the slightest suspicion that he was due to cross at Arnage he would have undoubtedly stopped there. All the same, the Company did not escape severe criticism just because one of their servants had erred. Referring to the method of working he said, 'It is certainly not a good, or an ordinary principle in railway working to rely on the attention, or the memory, of the engine drivers alone in such a matter'. And again, '. . . it will have been observed that the signals were lowered so as to allow MacDonald to run through Arnage, when he ought to have stopped there, and this was in accordance with the usual practice'. He thought it 'very necessary' that stationmasters should be responsible for exhibiting stop signals at crossing places, in addition to requiring drivers to obey the time-table instructions.

The Company's minutes record this but phrase it rather differently saying that Captain Tyler 'thought it advisable that the 'caution' signal at present used on the home signal should be converted into a 'danger' signal'.

The Board considered the report on 25th May and set up a committee consisting of the Chairman, Locomotive Superintendent, Superintendent of the line and the Engineer to look into the whole subject before coming to any final decisions. This committee's unrecorded recommendations were presented to the Finance, Works & Traffic Committee in August. In October, that body resolved that signals similar to those which had been installed at Arnage should be erected at the principal stations where trains cross and where the block system was in operation.

In conclusion the author's thanks are due to Mr Dawes of the Department of the Environment for kindly letting him see a copy of Captain Tyler's report.

In the report the driver's name is spelt McDonald, but in the appendices it is spelt MacDonald as well. – Ed.

At an accident at Maud Junction on 4th November 1970, a runaway train collided with a coal wagon at the goods yard buffers.

Courtesy North Eastern Press

LAST TRAINS – 4TH MAY 1965
by our Special Correspondent

The sky overhead was a clear, crisp, blue as I made my way into Peterhead Station. Under the station roof the still silent train waited and in the ticket office, the staff, perhaps thinking of the last run at Banff, were waiting expectantly. However, as time wore on, remarkably few people appeared and as the 'soulless green box on wheels' throbbed into life, the train was barely half full. At 3.20 p.m., No. D6152, and its train of two coaches and a parcels van, slowly pulled away from the platform and a small group of people watched the last passenger train leave Peterhead.

Each station along the line had its share of passengers getting on and off, but some fast running brought us to Maud on time. Some three minutes later the 'up Broch' arrived and after some shunting to pick up the parcels van, carried on to Aberdeen. After a wait of an hour, when I had time to survey the remains of the once busy rail centre, I joined the train for the return journey. With extra passengers from the 'down Aberdeen', we pulled away from Maud. As the brown Buchan landscape rolled by, my thoughts went back to the days of shiny green engines, smart coaches and passengers, of housewives, fishworkers, schoolchildren and tourists – the palmy days of yester-year.

It scarcely seemed anytime before it was all over and once again the train was sitting in the platform at Peterhead. The passengers slipped quietly away without any fuss and with them went 103 years of history.

Later in the evening, I journeyed north to witness the last run of the 'Bulger' where there was a completely different atmosphere. With the setting sun making the rails seems like red-hot bars, I watched the penultimate train near Cairnbulg. Already small groups of people could be seen at the trackside waiting for the last run of 'their' train. Indeed to some of the elderly locals, this is their train – paid for at £1 per household.

Just after 9 o'clock, I found myself in the company of a number of people at Fraserburgh Station. When the diesel unit arrived it was not long before it was filled to capacity. Before it left, I spoke to a couple who described life when the railway was opened. For them this last run was to be a nostalgic journey. Some ten minutes later, to the accompaniment of detonators and blaring horns, we left the 'Broch'. There was a gay holiday-like feeling about the train and with some retired railwaymen present, there was plenty of reminiscing. At each halt, a crowd gathered to pay their last respects and for much of the way the driver attempted a large number of variations on the two-tone horn.

At St. Combs, a large crowd had gathered, and after a short stop we started back for Fraserburgh amidst cheers and a blare of horns. It was dark now, and it was a sad train which made its way into Fraserburgh Station for the last time; sad, especially, for driver J. Murray, who was only four months short of 46 years service, to become redundant with the 8.25 p.m. Perhaps the occasion was best expressed by the couplet placed by one of the St. Combs villagers in the driver's cab:

'Farewell our Trainie, we shed a tear,
The Beeching axe has fallen here'.

Peterhead — No train timetable needed now!

G.N.S.R.A. Collection

Peterhead Station, after withdrawal of passenger services. The signal arms have been removed from their posts. The once busy goods yard has a ghost-like appearance.

Courtesy Frasers Studios, Peterhead

'BROCH' CLOSURE – 2ND OCTOBER 1965
by our 'Down' correspondent

A special cheap day return bought a train ride into sentiment, to be exact, a century of centiment and history. In April 1865 the 'Broch' section of the Formartine and Buchan Railway was opened and in October 1965, by courtesy of Dr Beeching, it was closed.

Unlike the Lossiemouth and Banff branches, there were two last trains. In consequence, the enthusiast had to choose either one train or choose two and change at Maud. I elected to take the last 'down' train and by 6.00 p.m. I was sitting in a compartment already more than half full. At 6.09 p.m. the last photographs were taken and the late final newspapers were being loaded into the guard's van. By now, the train was quite well filled and at 6.10 p.m. the last passenger train for Fraserburgh left the 'Joint' Station.

Kittybrewster, Dyce, Newmachar, and the other well known stations, each had their little crowd of sightseers and, by the time the train reached Ellon, it was quite dark. At Auchnagatt, a large crowd had gathered on the platform and, as we drew away, they were treated to a broadside of exploding detonators.

Maud was reached in time to see the last 'up' Aberdeen train from Fraserburgh. With the two trains on either side of the island platform, many passengers got out to view the proceedings and for five minutes the refreshment rooms did a roaring trade. The 'up' Aberdeen left and our train was shunted round to the vacated platform. By now I had found a comfortable place in the cab of the NBL diesel locomotive and got into conversation with the driver and fireman. It was from them that I discovered that they had both received redundancy notices and that this was the end of the road for them as well.

By the time we left Maud, we had fallen slightly behind time but some fast running kept us up to the mark. Leaving Strichen, I heard the story of how the vicious 1 in 66 incline which we were climbing sometimes brought the stream trains to a halt. The procedure then was to reverse back through Strichen, strictly against the regulations of course, then take a run at the incline. This usually did the trick and got it over the top.

From the cab windows could be seen little patches of light from open doors and liberal use was made of the horn to acknowledge the waves of the people. We rattled past Mormond Halt and under the dark invisible shape of the 'Stag' on Mormond Hill. All too soon Fraserburgh was approached and, as we rolled the last fifty yards under the awnings, a final defiant barrage of detonators echoed round the station. A small crowd of people was waiting at the barrier and slowly the passengers began to filter away. Small boys eagerly took away the bundles of newspapers and the last flashlight photographs were taken. The night air was now stilled; the train darkened and empty; the platform deserted. I turned and walked through the barrier – the last passenger to leave the platform at Fraserburgh.

Fraserburgh Station and shed, 25th January 1964.

C. Gammell

Our 'Up' correspondent reports:

At 18.36½ on 2nd October 1965, the last 'up' Buchan train made its sad journey from Fraserburgh to Aberdeen. After the usual photographs from the local press of the train, its crew, the passengers and the small crowd that had assembled to see it off, the six coach train left Fraserburgh. The mournful wail of the locomotive horn sounded a last long farewell to the 'Broch' as the last train set off on its 47 mile run.

As might be expected, the train was fuller than usual. Many of the locals had decided to travel on the last train out of, and the last train into Fraserburgh, changing, of course, at Maud where the two trains crossed. Nevertheless, the last train did do normal business as well. A family of three left the train at Rathen; three joined at Lonmay while eleven alighted at Strichen. At Maud things were most 'unusual'; the station had probably never been so crowded for years. Both last Buchan trains stood side by side. Hurriedly, the 'Brochers' detrained from the 'up' to the 'down' train, thus adding to the crowd of Maud inhabitants who had come to view the scene. The train had arrived 'three late' at Maud but it departed seven minutes behind time. Still, what did schedules matter on a night such as this! At Auchnagatt, the explosion of five detonators greeted the train's approach. This was Auchnagatt's very last passenger train. Before Maud we had been the last 'up' train but now we were 'the' last train. After picking up a few passengers, the train made its way to Arnage and thence to Ellon where about a dozen people had gathered to see the town's last train. So at Logierieve another correspondent joined the train and left the forsaken station in the pitch dark to the grunting of a pig and the cawing of the neighbouring rookery. Udny and Newmachar said farewell to rail passenger transport, and then came Dyce, soon to be a 'Junction' no more, and as quiet and desolate as usual. The passenger train clattered over the crossover on to the main line for the last time and made its way over the last few miles to Aberdeen to arrive somewhat late.

The era of the Buchan passenger trains had ended.

The last train from Fraserburgh was hauled by No. D6150; the last from Aberdeen by No. D6144.

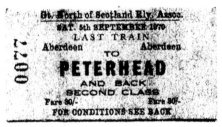

On Friday, 4th September 1970 the last freight train left Peterhead for Maud, while on the following Saturday a special train of two coaches took a party of enthusiasts over the line for the last time. The sun shone for quite a bit of the 'Farewell Excursion' which received considerable publicity in the Peterhead newspapers. The section Maud—Peterhead is now closed completely and while the solum of the line is left intact, the former station area at Peterhead has now been demolished and a new school and housing estate built on the site.

The Peterhead freight stands in Maud yard in 1970, a few weeks before the closure of the Peterhead to Maud section.

J. Morrison Collection

112

The first oil pipe-line train arrived at Maud Junction at 16.47 hrs. on Monday, 21st June 1976. Hundreds of tons of pipes were dealt with at Maud Junction for oilfield developments in the Peterhead and St. Fergus areas. A few days prior to the closure of the line, B R announced a further contract for the carriage of pipes for a land-line from St. Fergus, near Peterhead, to Teesside. Despite Local Authority pressure to retain the line for the carriage of these pipes, B R proceeded with the closure and ran the special trains to Inverurie where the pipes were carried overland to the Buchan area by lorry.

J. Morrison Collection

The last Peterhead freight stands at Maud Junction on 4th September 1970.

J. Morrison Collection

FORMARTINE & BUCHAN EXCURSION
DESCRIPTION OF THE ROUTE
by
A. W. Coutts

The Formartine and Buchan line to Fraserburgh and Peterhead originally takes its name from the two districts through which it passed. Aberdeenshire was divided into five districts which date back to medieval times and they are Mar, Garioch, Strathbogie, Formartine and Belhelvie. On the abolition of the feudal system, these districts were grouped together to form the county of Aberdeen. It should, of course, be noted that in the late sixteenth century the name Belhelvie was changed to Buchan but these general divisions of the county still remain to the present day. The two districts through which the railway runs is one remarkable for its agricultural character as well as for its historical and antiquarian interest.

The Formartine and Buchan Railway was sanctioned in 1858 and was opened as far as Mintlaw in July 1861 and was extended to Peterhead the following year. A branch was later built from Maud to Fraserburgh in 1865 and these lines, together with all the other lines in the north-east of Scotland, were grouped together to form, in 1866, the Great North of Scotland Railway. Its length from Dyce Junction, six miles north of Aberdeen, to Peterhead, is 38 miles and the branch from Maud to Fraserburgh is 16 miles in length. On this railtour we shall travel 120 miles and visit two of Aberdeenshire's most important towns.

The tour leaves the Joint Station at Aberdeen, and traces its way up the Denburn Valley passing the Union Terrace Gardens on the left and we enter Schoolhill Tunnel (230 yards long), passing the suburban station of Schoolhill, (where the tickets were collected), and continue into the larger Hutcheon Street Tunnel (270 yards), with the original Hutcheon Street Station at the north end. This section of line had encountered many difficulties and mishaps during its construction, not least of which was the collapse of part of the roof of the Hutcheon Street Tunnel which delayed construction of the line and it was not until 4th November 1867 that this section of track and the Joint Station was opened. The line continues past the Northern Co-operative premises at Berryden and we soon pass, the recently closed, Kittybrewster Station with its defunct motive power depot on the left and the disused goods yard on the right. After Kittybrewster, we pass the suburban stations of Don Street and Woodside where immediately below the now derelict station buildings we can see in the valley of the Don the now extensive woollen mills. The station at Persley can still be seen on the right as we race towards Bucksburn (originally spelt Buxburn), which was originally the station for the two large paper mills at Mugiemoss and Stoneywood, while to the west of the line, large granite quarries were to be found. Just before Bucksburn we can see the Twin Spires Creamery, now a principal source of employment in the area. After Bucksburn, Bankhead and Stoneywood (for Pirie's Mills), we continue on to Dyce which is the junction for the Buchan Railway. When the railway was opened, this place was a bleak moor but now it is a flourishing suburban village where the railway had depots for permanent way materials and other goods facilities.

To the left of the station we can see Dyce airport and, after leaving this impressive junction station, we can see, on the right, the modern factory of Lawson's of Dyce whose name is synonymous with good food. After Dyce, the River Don is crossed just before Parkhill Station and here to the right of the line is Parkhill House. From the station, (closed 3rd April 1950), we can see, on the left, the woods of Elrick and here the line suddenly climbs steeply at 1 in 74 in order to surmount Summerhill, the village of the same name being noted in the hollow on the left. New Machar, as the village is now called, four miles from Parkhill, is our next place of interest, and the station has a very fine view of the Deeside and Donside hills. Half a mile beyond the station we enter the deepest cutting on the line through the hill of Strypes. This cutting is almost a mile long and in some places is almost fifty feet in depth. As we emerge from it, the extensive and beautiful countryside opens up to view. The next station we pass through is Udny and this was originally the station for Udny Castle, Pitmedden and Haddo Houses. Udny Castle can still be seen towering above the surrounding trees as one approaches the station. At this point the proposed railway of the Earl of Aberdeen was to leave the main line and proceed through the grounds of Haddo House to Tarves and Methlick. On leaving Udny, we pass, on the right, the farms of Monkshill and Orchardston and, on the left, that of Cloisterseat. Logierieve, originally called Newburgh Road, the next station on the line, was originally placed in a moss but due to the skilful cultivation of the farmers, this has long since disappeared. The next station was Esslemont, (closed 15th September 1952), which was originally built to serve Esslemont House, situated about one mile north of the station, and on leaving the station we pass through a very deep cutting through the hill of Woolaw and we cross the Ythan by a bridge of four arches over fifty feet above the stream. Although we do not wish to alarm the passengers, it should be remembered that the first Ythan Bridge fell down in 1861 owing to some undue pressure on the central arch supports. This accident did, in fact, delay the opening of the line by several months and even then, great anxiety was caused to the locals by the passage of the first train.

The station at Ellon was rebuilt about 1895, in preparation for the opening of the line to Boddam which took place on 2nd August 1897, and helped to link the isolated communities of the area for thirty-five years until its eventual closure to passenger traffic on 31st October 1932. The station consisted of three platforms, two serving the main line and one for the 15½ mile long branch which linked Auchmacoy, Pitlurg, Hatton, Cruden Bay, Longhaven and Boddam. Ellon, in later years, served a large area due to the closing of this line. This market town is situated on the banks of the Ythan and it is this river which is celebrated for its mussel pearls *(Mya Margaritifera)*. Even with the closure of the railway, the town continues to thrive as an important marketing centre in the north-east of Scotland. After Ellon, we pass Auchterellon, on the left, and through a heavy cutting through what used to be called the Gallow Hill. Since crossing the river Ythan, we have been in the Buchan district of Aberdeenshire and approaching Arnage we get some idea of the hilly area which is central Buchan. On the right of the station is Arnage House which is not visible from the railway, but the towers of which used to be visible for an instant on passing. It is beautifully situated, surrounded by fine thriving woods. The village of Arnage is over a quarter of a mile from the station. On leaving, the line passes on through the bleak Buchan moorland which is of little interest being, for the most part, desolate. Auchnagatt consisted of a wayside inn and a meal mill before the coming of the railway. Now, because of it, there is a nucleus of a small village of substantial houses. Auchnagatt was the station for the whole area. From here we enter a wild and picturesque ravine under the farm of Altnaud. Our first stop on this railtour is Maud Junction which is 31 miles from Aberdeen and here the railway bifurcates, the line on the left going to Fraserburgh and, on the right to Peterhead. The station, of four platforms, which has refreshment facilities, has been variously named Banks, Brucklay and Maud in the course of its chequered career. The name of the village is Bank and when the line was opened in 1861 there were only two thatched cottages here, but now Maud Junction is a village of considerable size.

Proceeding along the Peterhead line we pass the ruins of the old Clackrish Castle and continue past the Hill of Parkhouse with its fine Druidical Circle. On the right is Aikey Brae, renowed for its annual fair while, on the left, is the Abbey of Deer which at one time had its own platform. We continue along until we reach the station of Mintlaw and Old Deer (now Mintlaw). Half a mile east of the station is Mintlaw, a small country village, situated at the crossing of the old Aberdeen and Fraserburgh turnpike road with that from Peterhead to Banff. From Mintlaw to Longside the line passes a succession of small farms and crofts and on approaching Longside, we skirt, on our left, the woods of Ardlawhill and soon pass the quiet station situated on the north bank of the Ugie River. The village lies about half a mile to the right of the station and the river separates the two. Situated on rising ground, the central point is a huge parish church. A little beyond the station we pass Millbank and, looking to the left, we get a glimpse of the once eminent manufactory at Millbank celebrated for its fine cloth. It stood between the two Ugies, just west of their confluence, was a major source of employment in the area, and was closed in 1828; now it is deserted. The river, however, is crossed a little below this by a skew girder bridge of three spans, each of 31 ft. Newseat, the next station on the line, was, up to the 1890s, a mere platform, but the station was later extended and indeed this station is one of the rare examples, on the whole of the 'Great North', of two storey premises. Our next 'port of passing' is Inverugie, which is but two miles from Peterhead, but the loop has long since vanished. Originally, this station was built to serve a number of 'select suburban villas' but now it is just desolate farm land with a bleak outlook on the surrounding territory. Peterhead, the terminus of the branch, stands upon a peninsula projecting into the North Sea and is, in fact, the most easterly part of Scotland. At Peterhead, the signal box was on our right as we enter the two platformed station, and on our left we can see the old goods yard and engine shed. This is our second stop and here lunch will be served. There was a steeply graded harbour branch which has long since been out of use. Although the Boddam branch terminated about three miles south of Peterhead, there were no plans for extending it. There was, however, a private line from Stirlinghill above Boddam to Peterhead. The prisoners travelled to work at the quarries on it and the granite was transported down to the south breakwater.

Back at Maud, we may observe the signal box, now closed, on the right, and on our left, the goods shed and the turntable pit. Maud North box can just be discerned at the north end of the island platform. The line runs north climbing until Brucklay Station, 1¾ miles from Maud. For almost two miles the line climbs and then drops sharply into Strichen. On this stretch the trains manage to get up a good speed. The village is situated on the banks of the North Ugie near the western foot of Mormond Hill. This is a heather-clad hill rising to 796 ft. On the south-west brow of the mound, there is a figure of a horse cut out in turf occupying a space of nearly half an acre and filled in with white quartz of which the hill is mainly composed. On the corresponding south-east slope, a figure of a stag is outlined. Above the white horse there stands the gaunt ruins of an old hunting lodge with 'Rab Gibb Commands' cut out above the door. A fact of interest is that before Strichen had a parish church of its own, the people had to cross the Hill of Mormond to Rathen and the footpath is traceable to this day. There was, at one time, a cairn on the hill called the 'resting cairn', where, on the occasion of funerals, they rested the coffin before climbing the rest of the hill. Leaving Strichen, the line skirts the southern base of Mormond and we soon pass the local station of that name which served scattered farms and crofts as well as facilitating climbers and walkers wishing to reach the eastern brow of the hill. The station building is similar to that at Newseat. We soon pass Lonmay and, at one time, this was a station for several important houses in the district. Between the station and the sea lies the Loch of Strathbeg (original spelt Strabeg), a sheet of water covering some 550 acres. From Rathen Station, 2½ miles from Lonmay, the ruins of the Castle of Inverallochy may still be seen to the east, now bare and desolate. The line continues across flat ground towards Philorth (originally a private station for Lord Saltoun), which is a one platform station almost on the outskirts of Fraserburgh.

After crossing the Water of Philorth, just before Philorth Station, the line continues towards Fraserburgh, the northerly terminus of the line and also the junction for the former light railway to Cairnbulg and St. Combs. At Fraserburgh we can see, on our right, the trackbed of the light railway and on our left, we can see the sidings into the Consolidated Pneumatic Tool Company's factory. The terminal station consists of three platforms with an extensive booking hall but unfortunately these now lie derelict and desolate. A two road engine shed with turntable existed to the west of the station where the remains can still be seen. The goods yard is to the east and is still served by British Railways for the daily freight train to Aberdeen. A famous Fraserburgh landmark can still be seen, that of the Fraserburgh South Parish Church, to the west, above the station. The station buildings were erected in 1903 and are similar to those at Elgin with which it is often confused. Aboyne, Banchory and Inverurie were also reconstructed in a similar style.

We now return direct to Aberdeen and call at the stations for photographic purposes. Much of the material for this description of the route has been based on W. Ferguson's *Guide to The Great North of Scotland Railway* published in 1881. Mr Ferguson, who resided at Kinmundy, south of Mintlaw, was Chairman of the 'Great North' from 1879 until his death in 1904. He was known by his patronymic, *Kinmundy*, an expression of esteem which he deeply appreciated. (Wm. B. Ferguson was the Secretary from 1868 until 1880). Kinmundy House was built in 1734 and is interesting as a specimen of the house of that period, being formed by a centre to the south and two wings to the north, connected by a curtain wall thus forming a court. Now nothing is left of the house or the family.

Where possible, the description has been brought up to date, but changes in modern times are rapid in many instances. Several of the stations are being demolished. Very little is left of Parkhill while Elrick box can only be located by its mileage from Aberdeen (8m 1,502 yd). Part of the platform has been demolished at Newmachar while the footbridge and 'up' platform buildings have gone. At Udny the 'down' platform coping and the buildings have been removed and, as at Newmachar, the signal boxes have been demolished. Logierieve has been boarded and the box (closed 1894) has recently been moved. Esslemont has been converted into a dwelling house, the 'up' platform, out of use since 1925, can be discerned. The up to date position at the other stations is not certain; many of the footbridges have been removed while many of the smaller buildings, including the signal boxes, have been removed.

The line was single except for a short section from Parkhill to Elrick which was doubled from 1920 until 1925. During the winter months, these boxes were closed and the section Dyce–Newmachar was one single line block section. There were passing loops at Newmachar, Udny, Logierieve, Esslemont, Ellon, Arnage, Auchnagatt, Maud, Mintlaw, Longside, Inverugie, Brucklay, Strichen, Lonmay and Rathen. Those at Logierieve, Inverugie and Rathen were taken out in 1894 although the signal cabins remained long after. Esslemont loop was the next to be removed in 1925 while arrangements were made 'to switch out' the loops at Mintlaw and Brucklay. In the last few years all the loops, except at Maud, have been removed. The line is now operated in three sections; Dyce–Maud, Maud–Peterhead and Maud–Fraserburgh. There are two trains, Monday to Friday, one to Peterhead and one to Fraserburgh, while on Saturday, there is one to Fraserburgh.

The Buchan lines have been closed to passenger trains (1965) and it is only a matter of time until the freight trains cease to run. Today's tour may be the last passenger train over the lines — time will tell. We hope that you have enjoyed the excursion.

FORMARTINE & BUCHAN EXCURSION
by
Alister W. Coutts

By 10.00 hrs the assembled party was comfortably seated and waiting for the departure to come. The weeks of preparation were beginning to bear fruit and the train departed on time (typical practice prior to modern times). From Aberdeen, the train rapidly sped on its northerly course passing through the suburbs of the capital of the north-east. The train consisted of No. D5328 and four coaches, and was filled by over 150 enthusiastic travellers. The fourth coach was added at the last minute to cope with the demand.

By 10.10 Dyce Junction had been reached and passed and the supply of *Press* and *Journals* had been exhaused by the passengers, all wishing to read the excellent article on the Buchan lines which was the centre-piece of the newspaper. In wintry conditions, the train continued on its non-stop run to Udny where the station had been newly painted and decorated with bunting. Here, the Earl of Haddo and the Laird of Udny boarded with great dignity — in 'Great North' tradition. From here the sun began to shine and an unscheduled stop was made at Ellon for technical purposes. The photographers made use of it to record the scene. From here the diesel locomotive had to run on reduced power.

At Maud Junction another photographic stop resulted in our late departure for Peterhead and many of the 'tourists' were sceptical of our chances of reaching Peterhead on time. None of these sceptics, however, would admit to their reason for anxiety, but it was rumoured that many were feeling great pangs of hunger and a resultant empty gaping void. The refreshment room at Maud Junction had been closed!

They need not have worried for we arrived on time to an enthusiastic welcome by Provost Edward Duncan, and a guide book was presented to each member of the party along with cream of chicken (or tomato) soup. Our dinner, which was provided by the generous hospitality of Crosse & Blackwell, continued with London Grill, complete with mushrooms, and the trimmings. For our third course we were presented with the choice of a mixed fruit pudding or a golden sponge pudding and this was topped by Nestle's cream. For our last course, rolls, cheese and coffee were the order of the day.

More photographs followed dinner and the train continued back to Maud after stopping at all the intermediate stations. The Provost joined the party,

FORMARTINE & BUCHAN EXCURSION

TIMETABLE

Mileage						
M	C					
—	—	ABERDEEN	1000			1715
		Schoolhill				
		Hutcheon St.				
1	29	Kittybrewster				
		Don Street				
		Woodside				
		Persley				
4	5	Bucksburn				
		Bankhead				
		Stoneywood				
6	18	DYCE	(1010)			1705†
7	29	Parkhill				
8	68	Elrick				
11	32	NEWMACHAR				1643†
14	32	UDNY				1632†
16	19	LOGIERIEVE				1623†
17	58	Esslemont				
19	26	ELLON				1612†
23	4	ARNAGE				1559†
26	57	AUCHNAGATT				1546†
30	75	MAUD	arr. 1100			1538†
			dep. 1110		1320 arr.	
35	8	MINTLAW			1310†	
38	20	LONGSIDE			1259†	
40	54	NEWSEAT			1248†	
42	00	INVERUGIE			1240†	
44	10	PETERHEAD	arr. 1140		1230 dep.	
30	75	MAUD		dep. 1327		arr. 1533
32	64	BRUCKLAY				1529†
36	62	STRICHEN				1516†
39	14	MORMOND				1506†
41	58	LONMAY				1456†
44	6	RATHEN				1446†
45	45	PHILORTH				1438†
46	79	FRASERBURGH	arr. 1400			dep.1430

† arrives five minutes earlier; mileages from Aberdeen total 120m 28c

A BR Sulzer Type 2 locomotive stands at Peterhead Station on 24th May 1969, with the 'Formartine & Buchan Excursion'.

Courtesy Crosse & Blackwell

The 'Formartine & Buchan Excursion' draws to a halt beneath the overall roof of a gloomy Peterhead Station on 24th May 1969.

G.N.S.R.A. Collection

as did the Manager, Mr G. E. Copeman, of Crosse & Blackwell's, who left at Inverugie.

From here to Fraserburgh, good timekeeping was again maintained, although little of the time, lost over the meal at Peterhead, was made up. The Civic Dignitaries were out to greet the train and once again the members of the party were presented with brochures about the 'Broch'. Many of the passengers went in to view the town and visit several of its highlights for refreshments. Indeed, one of the committee members was so taken with the town and its gracious occupants that the train departed without him and his friend. They did not regain the confines of the 'Express' until the stop at Strichen. Stops were made at all the intermediate stations except Esslemont and Parkhill.

At Udny the Laird left the train and followed it to Aberdeen with his Bentley.

In fact, it is a tribute to the railwaymen that the train did not arrive back at Aberdeen more than a few moments late. Several passengers had indicated a desire to catch the 5.15 p.m. train to Glasgow, and this was, in fact, achieved. The alighting passengers took a last look at the train with its resplendent headboard and carriage destination boards. From the favourable reaction to the tour we are sure that the result will be an increased demand for more tours run by the Association.

'The Northern Belle' at Fraserburgh. Probably the longest passenger train to run from the 'Broch', and this, after termination of regular services.

J. Morrison Collection

THE LAST FREIGHT TO FRASERBURGH
by
Lewis McAllan

At 06.45 hrs on Friday, 5th October 1979, several of our members assembled at the 'Shell' in Aberdeen Joint Station and, joined by an equal number from the Brechin Preservation Society and two pressmen, we made our way to platform 9, to board (by special arrangement with BR) the last scheduled freight train on the Buchan line, which, despite the usual representations in such circumstances, was to close on the following day. It was a grey, murky, foggy morning and on the previous day, the Aberdeen area had had the highest rainfall since records began − 3.6 inches in 24 hours!

In due course locomotive No. 27 020 appeared with two bogie vehicles, (for the parcels and us), and set back to collect ten vanfits, one coal wagon (all loaded) and a rear brake van. At 07.12 hrs we departed, with, in the cab, driver Fred Smith, relief driver Dick Anderson and Traction Inspector Bill Duncan. Guard Norman Thomson held the fort in the brake van. We also had with us, unofficially, the chief Passenger Trains Inspector for the Scottish Region, who proved equally adept at keeping an eye on freight trains. So we were well looked after.

With the 'train staff' collected at Dyce signal box, we were in sole possession of all 40½ miles of the Buchan branch. Outside, it was water, water everywhere, − the swollen Don at Parkhill and lochs, great and small, in all the hollows of the land.

Now would come the climb to Newmachar, with a total load estimated, by Inspector Duncan, at 460 tonnes and on probably greasy rails. Someone produced a gradient profile showing 1 in 80/75 all the way to the Newmachar Summit. 'It looks like Annapurna', said one of the pressmen.

About half-way up, we gradually came to a halt; the rails were indeed greasy. Thinking of all the other Buchan banks to come, we felt we would be out on a day, and not the expected half-day, trip. That was a fine feeling − we were ready for anything. With sand applied, driver Smith managed to move forward inch by inch. Several times the process had to be repeated − stop, sand and away − until we were over the top. The journey between mileposts 10¼ and 12 had taken 75 minutes. Kingseat Hospital had been in view, dimly through the haar, for so long that one began to wonder whether some obscure magnetic force was drawing us to it.

At Udny yard the sole remaining link with the past was the loading gauge, still standing lonely just outside the new housing estate. At Ellon, the River Ythan looked more like the Mississipi. Charging on through the station, we heard the throttle opened for the next 1 in 75 bank to Arnage and this time there was no problem. After an unscheduled stop (reason unknown) near the point where the Auchnagatt 'down' home signal would once have stood, we pulled up in the Maud loop at 09.49 hours.

The Fraserburgh to Aberdeen freight at Maud in 1979.

J. Morrison Collection

A Fraserburgh to Aberdeen freight train pictured near Maud in 1977. Traffic had dwindled to a van of parcels, two fish containers for Billingsgate and a returned empty oil tank from Swansons of Fraserburgh. Maud Junction remained the busiest station on the line, handling large quantities of fertilizers and animal feed for Buchan agricultural merchants in addition to pipes for the oil industry.

G. O'Hara

Shunting at Fraserburgh yard in 1949. Note the giant driving wheels of the G N S R 4-4-0 locomotive.

J. Morrison Collection

Sandy Simmers, P. W. Inspector on the Buchan Line, at Maud Junction yard in 1979.

J. Morrison Collection

The vanfits and coal wagon were all for Maud and were detached. The engine and coaching vehicles ran forward into the station, of which the passengers made a thorough exploration and where a press photograph was taken of the whole company alongside the engine. Most of the Maud traffic was gravity shunted into the yard, under the eye of leading railman, Jim Morrison, but, in the end, driver Smith had to set back and help.

At 10.23 hrs Maud was left, with a load reduced to the two bogies and the brake van. At 'Strichen Toon' the school classrooms were brightly lit against the gloom. A short blast from the horn and pupils looked up from their desks; a forst of little hands rose in a collective salutation.

Mormond Summit was tackled in fine style, but where was Mormond Hill? With excess of modesty, she had completely covered herself, unable to bear the thought of looking for the last time at what she had seen so often for more than a century. Down through Lonmay, Rathen and Philorth and the loop outside, Fraserburgh was reached at 10.50 hrs.

The engine came round and, after sending the brake van into a siding, propelled the two bogie vehicles into the main goods platform road, where we alighted. Until we arrived, the yard had been occupied by one coal wagon. The return journey commenced at 11.45 hrs. With the brake van left behind, we consisted of engine and two vehicles. The intention was to make a non-stop run to Dyce.

As we left, there was the sound of detonators; at Strichen more waves from the schoolchildren; at Maud more detonators. With her limited load, locomotive No. 27 020 made short work of the gradients, and all went well through Brucklay, Esslemont and Logierieve and all those other places with names evocative of what had been. But suddenly, on the descent from Newmachar, there was an unexpected brake application. Someone looked out and cried, 'Oh! There's a man with a red flag'.

What had happened? Had the elements at last caught up with us? Had the Parkhill Viaduct collapsed in the flood? Were we marooned, fated, Flying Dutchman-like, to travel for ever up and down the Buchan?

Not quite. True, there had been a small subsidence somewhere near Parkhill but we could proceed with caution.

We reached Dyce at 13.11 hrs and after a few minutes waiting for the 'road', we finally left the Buchan and drew up at platform 8 in Aberdeen at 13.29 hrs. We had enjoyed a smooth and comfortable run and a memorable outing.

So fare ye well, ye Mormond Braes! When again will you be seen from a train?

THE BUCHAN LINE — SIGNAL BOX CLOSURES

Arnage 5/1/65	Auchnagatt 6/7/66	Boddam 29/6/36
Brucklay 15/6/59	Cruden Bay 24/1/32	Elrick 23/8/25
Ellon North 16/5/32	Ellon South 18/10/67	Esslemont 23/8/25
Fraserburgh 27/6/66	Longside North 5/11/18	Longside South 10/12/65
Lonmay 5/1/65	Maud North 21/7/35	Maud South 5/3/69
Mintlaw North 23/10/27	Mintlaw South 15/6/59	Newmachar 9/12/65
Parkhill 23/8/25	Peterhead 17/5/66	Pitlurg 24/1/32
Strichen 27/6/66	Udny North 16/12/01	Udny South 29/6/66

The interior of Maud signal box, 1968.

J. Morrison Collection

LINE CLOSURES

Line	Closed to passengers	Closed to freight
Boddam line	31/10/32	7/11/45
Peterhead line	3/5/65	7/9/70
Fraserburgh line	4/10/65	6/10/79
St. Combs line	3/5/65	3/5/65

NOTES AND NEWS

The November issue went to press not long after the closure of the Buchan line. Both before the actual date (Saturday, 6th October 1979) and after, there were various attempts to postpone and to stop the closure; then there were attempts to take over the line privately. However, the lifting of the line has been going on at a steady pace. Work started at Lonmay with the intention of completing the more remote section before the onset of severe winter weather. At the time of writing, we are uncertain of what has been completely lifted, but it is possible that work is progressing in more than one area. The rails in the vicinity of Ellon Station have been lifted and it is possible that these are the rails which BR wish to recover for use elsewhere.

An engine went to Fraserburgh on Tuesday, 23rd October, to recover the wagons which had been taken up on the last 'official' train on 5th October. It is possible that other trains have been on the branch in connection with the recovery of the 'redundant assets'. A number of assets have been recovered from the contracts for use at the Alford Station museum complex, including such items as pens, ledgers, ink stands etc.

In the latter part of December, we understand that a meeting was held in the Baron's Hotel, Auchnagatt, with a view to running steam trains on the Dyce—Maud section of the line. We have been unable to find any press notices of this meeting and any details of progress would be welcome.

In the local newspapers in November and December there appeared an advertisement of full page width, and about 8 inches high. This was a cartoon strip — really two strips, with five sections in each — surrounded by a railway track. Along the top was 'The end of the Line?' and along the bottom was 'The start of a new one!' Two characters, Graham and Sandy, were discussing the problems of a small road haulage company handling 600 tonnes a week — 'but that's more than the Buchan line handled!' with the reply in the last frame 'Sssh! Don't tell everyone!'. We are not sure what the aim of the advert really was. They may have been trying to sell the idea of transhipping rail-borne goods at Aberdeen or Inverurie for Buchan at a cheaper rate than when the Buchan line was in operation. One of the occasions the advert appeared was in the *Press* and *Journal* on 12th December.

Although the bridge over the road at Lonmay has no track on it, its height can be a headache for some lorries. In the early hours of 7th January, it ripped off the roof of a lorry carrying polystyrene fish trays which were scattered all around. The road was closed for several hours as workmen cleared up the debris.

THE PORT ERROLL RAILWAY
A miniature memory

In the thick of closures and abandonment of railways in Buchan, it will be heartening to railway enthusiasts to know that, in the year following the final closure, a new miniature narrow gauge style railway was opened to the public in the Cruden Bay area. Known as the Port Erroll Railway, the line boasts steam power which has proved a magnet to enthusiasts, tourists and the local public alike.

Like many early railways, the first proposals to build the line were met with some conservationist opposition by those who feared the ruin of a scenic amenity area. Fortunately, the majority saw the advantages of the project in revitalizing the village of Cruden Bay for the attraction of holiday-makers and tourists. After all, the original standard gauge line had been built for that purpose.

The railway follows a scenic route from the centre of the village down a wooded valley to an inlet from the sea at the foot of Slains Castle. The valley has historical connections with the author, Bram Stoker, of *Dracula* fame, who spent regular holidays in Cruden Bay at the turn of the century. There are three stations on the line, Port Erroll, in the village centre, Burnside Halt, serving a wooded area adjacent to a small river, and Smugglers Bay which is the location of Bram Stoker's novel, *The Mystery of the Sea*.

The railway is built to capture the atmosphere of a typical rural branch line and is open during the summer months from April to the end of October. Although all the standard gauge lines are gone, the bark of a hard working steam locomotive hauling a crowded miniature passenger train can be heard echoing through this small Buchan Valley. The railway is, indeed, an oasis in this now rail-less desert.

The 2.30 p.m. Sunday afternoon train coasts downhill from Burnside Halt with a full load of passengers for Smugglers Bay.

A. Sangster Collection

The author, on his locomotive, *Donald*, which is named after his five year old son, at Port Erroll. The model is of an American 4-4-0 of the 1860s and is on display at Smugglers Bay Railway Museum.

Courtesy Aberdeen Journals

Donald, after arrival at Port Erroll with a train from Smugglers Bay.

Courtesy Aberdeen Journals

Port Erroll Station, together with engine shed. Diesel locomotive *Elizabeth* stands outside the shed.

A. Sangster Collection

Approaching Smugglers Bay, 'Romulus' 0-6-0, *Donald* steams in from Port Erroll.

A. Sangster Collection

EPITAPH

On 21st November 1980, about one hundred former employees of the Buchan lines gathered in the Station Hotel at Ellon for their second annual reunion dinner and dance. This reunion is the last thread and link of their former comradeship, loyalty and love of the line. All are 'old school' railwaymen, who gave the years of their working lives in total to the railway. They are the unsung heroes who gave dedicated and long service, often for moderate or poor financial return, yet, given the opportunity, would go out and do the same thing tomorrow.

As a result of an announcement by Occidental Oil, that they were planning to build an ethylene plant near Peterhead, the Grampian Regional Council, recognising the possible future need for rail transport in the area, purchased the solum of the line from Dyce to Fraserburgh for the grand total of one penny. This purchase, which was effected in December 1980, puts the onus on the local authority to maintain the track bed in a condition that would facilitate the immediate re-laying of the line should justifiable traffic materialize. It is believed that the council would be interested in either British Rail or a private company reopening the railway.

It will be very interesting to see if heavy diesel-hauled freights will once again 'growl' their way through the landscape of Buchan.

In the three years that have passed since the Grampian Regional Council undertook the ownership of the trackbed, a number of changes have taken place which is determining the future of the line. The Chemical-Petroleum Plant planned by Occidental Oil in Peterhead was shelved and with steady decay of the route fences and stations setting in, Grampian Region, being realistic in understanding there was little prospect of the line reopening in a conventional form, convened a committee to report on the remains of the railway. The committee proposed that parts of the line should be turned over for leisure and recreational use such as country walks and pony trekking, etc.,

The author is currently negotiating with the Regional Council to take over the Maud Junction to Mintlaw section of the route to construct a 15 in. narrow gauge railway which would serve the tourist attractions of the ancient Abbey of Deer and Aden Country Park and Agricultural Museum. The line will be called the West Buchan Railway and it is hoped to have stage one of the project, from Mintlaw to Deer Abbey, open for the summer of 1984. Diesel multiple units have been designed for the new line by Messrs Severn-Lamb of Stratford-upon-Avon.

Meanwhile, the Port Erroll Railway has been upgraded from a 7¼ in. to a 15 in. gauge line and will operate in its new larger improved state from Easter 1983. Buchan will therefore be served by two narrow gauge lines covering contrasting areas of tourist attraction.